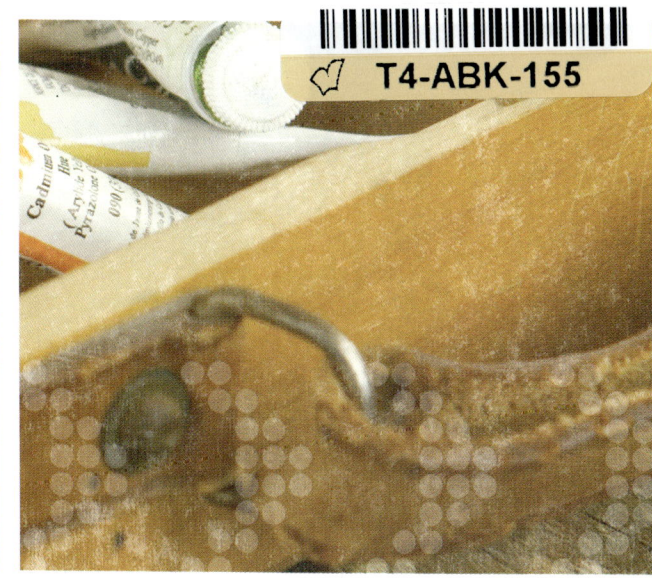

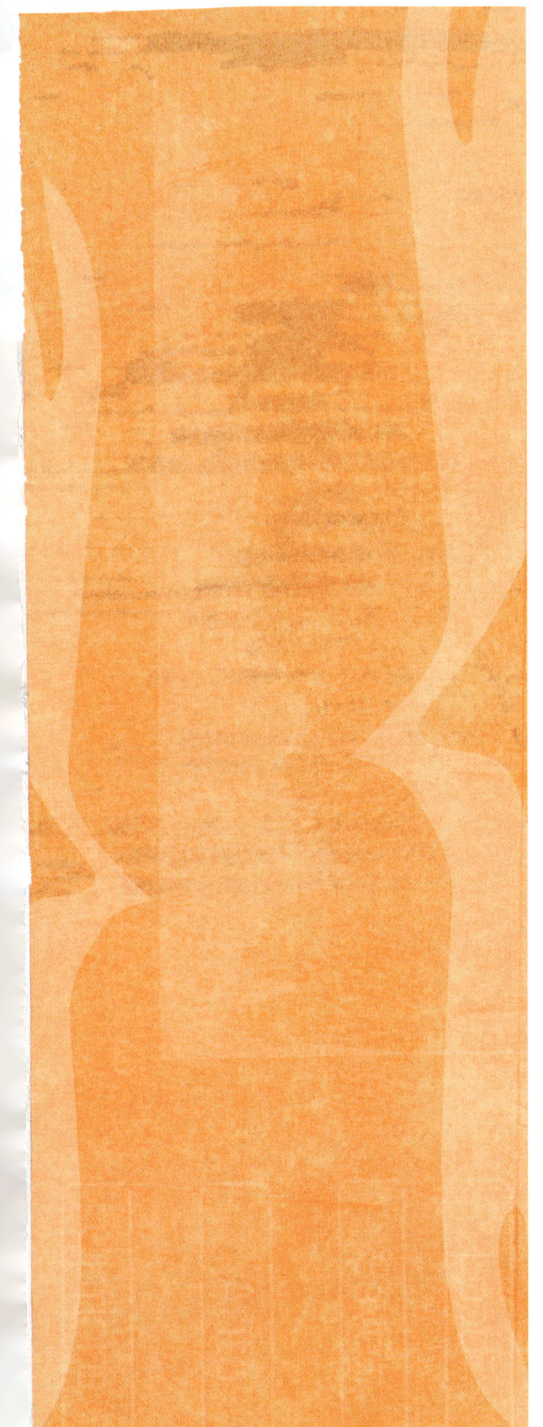

creativity:

Take the obvious, add a cupful of brains...stir well and bring to a boil.
—Bernard M. Baruch

Baruch's recipe for creativity is exactly what you need to get started into the art of digital scrapbooking.

While you may not think of the computer as providing a means for art, it can be. Creating digital layouts provides as much opportunity for creativity, invention and design as do traditional layouts. It's simply that the tools are different. Digital layouts are just another medium for expression, and those layouts can incorporate a wide range of elements and effects.

You may think digital layouts equal: blocky type, black and white, poor-quality printouts, but that's not true. Instead, you can create free-flowing, artistic layouts from simple to complex. In fact, you have available all the features of a paper-based layout plus the unique aspects of working digitally. You can easily make changes, alter and repair photographs, merge images and more. This book is your starting place; here you'll find tools, advice, design ideas and everything you need to explore this new world of scrapbooking.

So be courageous and daring and add a pinch of your imagination as you venture into this new medium of scrapbooking.

Each of us is an artist, capable of conceiving and creating a vision from the depths of our being.

Dorothy Fadiman

The Artists of Autumn Leaves
(Top to Bottom, Left to Right)

Rhonna Farrer | Tracy Kyle | Lisa Russo | Tina Barriscale
Joanna Bolick | Nia Reddy | Traci Turchin | Veronica Ponce
Anna Aspnes | Rhonda Stark | Anne Langpap
Gina Cabrera | Laura Vanderbeek | Dena Simoneaux
Jeri Ingalls | Erin Trimble | Shelley O'Hara | Chris Ford

TABLE OF
CONTENTS

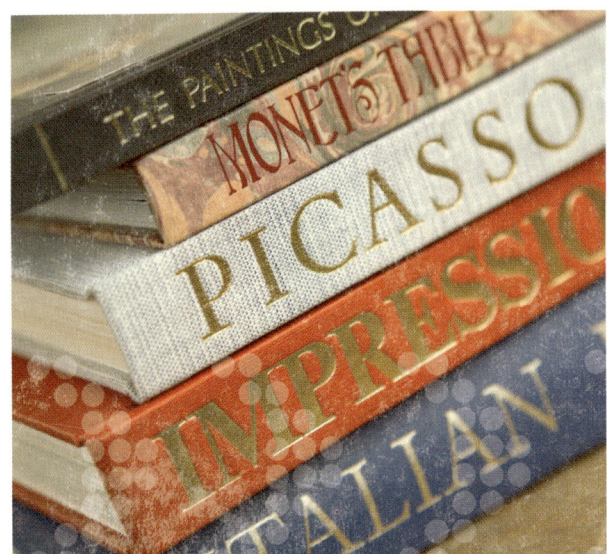

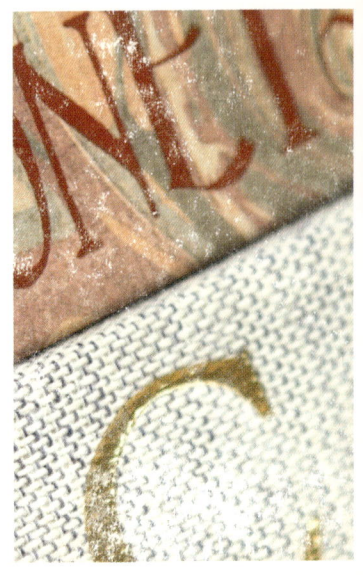

CHAPTER ONE
BASICS 6-13

CHAPTER TWO
TOOL BAR 14-21

CHAPTER THREE
CUSTOM BRUSHES 22-31

CHAPTER FOUR
LIGHT MODES 32-37

CHAPTER FIVE
FILTERS 38-45

CHAPTER SIX
ELEMENTS 46-55

CHAPTER SEVEN
OVERLAYS 56-65

CHAPTER EIGHT
GALLERY 66-79

CHAPTER ONE
BASICS

As Aesop commented, "Little by little does the trick." The same is true with going digital. You don't have to be an expert to get started; you can learn little by little, step by step. For instance, start incorporating digital elements into paper-based layouts, printing out altered photographs, images or paper and attaching them to "regular" layouts. As you learn more about how to work with different elements, you can expand your skills so eventually you know how to build entirely digital layouts. Don't be intimidated—just get started!

A work of art which did not begin in emotion is not art.

—Paul Cezanne

portrait of a little boy

In Cole's world there are endless treasures to be found and collected. Whereas a walk in the stroller is fast-paced and aerobic, a walk with trike and son leading the way moves at a much slower pace. From rocks and wood to interesting bits of dirt, we make our way slowly down the roads of the neighborhood, pausing more often that I would prefer, but enjoying our afternoons that much more. To Cole this is is world, and to me, this is my son. 10.24.04

CuRioSiTy

cuffed jeans that are just a little too long

pedals that have yet to be used since you insist on shuffling instead

rocks, rocks, and more rocks

a piece of wood collected with care

yet another rock

a mandatory pitstop at a manhole cover

Road Trip

01

Road Trip
By Joanna

Emphasize the text on a page with drop shadows.

Living
By Tracy

Include a variety of photos in a layout by creating a photo collage in your photo editing program.

she's LIVING

Isabella is such a daredevil. She is fearless and she will try anything once. She is fulll of spunk and determination. We are just so very different.

I rarely stray from the main road. Routines and lists keep me sane. I am most happy at home. We are indeed so different. However, I find that spending each day with her is beginning to change me. I follow along with her, joining in on her adventurers, and finding out that maybe her way is truly living life to its fullest.

Calm Before the STORM

Just look at this sweet face - on the verge of a two year old toddler's meltdown. On this particular day you were watching the boys riding their bikes and having fun. By this time your cousin's scooter was looking like a mighty fine object to take for spin around the block. I happily obliged and chaperoned your highly anticipated journey. Everything was going just peachy until you made continuous attempts to outrun me. The fact that we were near the road left me no choice but to do the unthinkable...take the scooter away! Noooooo! Fortunately, the tears did not last too long and I remain in your good graces for another day.

Storm
By Gina

Customize a slide mount with depth and texture that matches your layout.

Taylor
By Anne

Apply a drop shadow to any paper piece, text or element to give the illusion of depth.

- energetic
- dramatic
- playful
- emotional
- artistic
- passionate
- vivacious
- curious
- hilarious

Yes, you are!

Taylor...

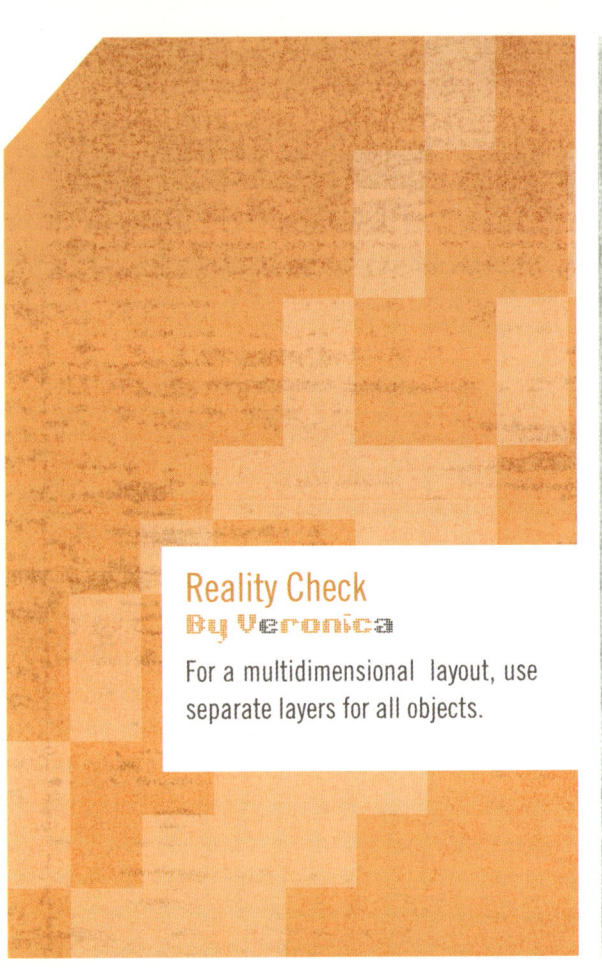

Reality Check
By Veronica

For a multidimensional layout, use separate layers for all objects.

courtesy of my five-year-old

realitycheck

- what a 26 year age gap can do -

GIANCARLO: Mom, tell me about the old days.
MOM: The old days?
GIANCARLO: Yeah, you know, when you were a kid.
MOM: Okay, well what would you like to know?
GIANCARLO: Did you have telephones and televisions?
MOM: Well, yeah, we did. But we didn't have the Internet.
GIANCARLO: Wow, that must have been a really long time ago.

MAGNIFICO MEXICO

{2003-2005}

- ARTE
- COCINA
- CULTURA
- HISTORIA
- LENGUAJE
- ASOMBROSO

MOM & DAD HAVE BEEN LIVING IN MEXICO FOR ALMOST TWO YEARS...WE GET TO HEAR ALL OF THE STORIES, ADVENTURES & WILL BE VISITING SOON. IT HAS BEEN SUCH A TREAT TO LIVE SO MANY ADVENTURES VICARIOUSLY. MOM & DAD, YOU ARE ALL OF OUR HEROES!

MEXICO

Magnifico Mexico
By Rhonna

Add lines of various widths and colors to the shapes in your layout to make them "pop" off the page.

Better Things
By Lisa
Make text stand out by creating text boxes with different type colors or effects.

"Can't we just talk about the better things in life?!"

Ocean
By Laura
Give photos a "digital mat" by drawing inside borders to separate background papers from the photos.

enjoying the crash of the Ocean Waves

Taking time to enjoy the ocean was a huge priority on our list of things to do in hawaii this year. Watching Gavin and his Dad surf for the first time together was worth the entire trip!

hawaiian memories 12.13.2004

11

b

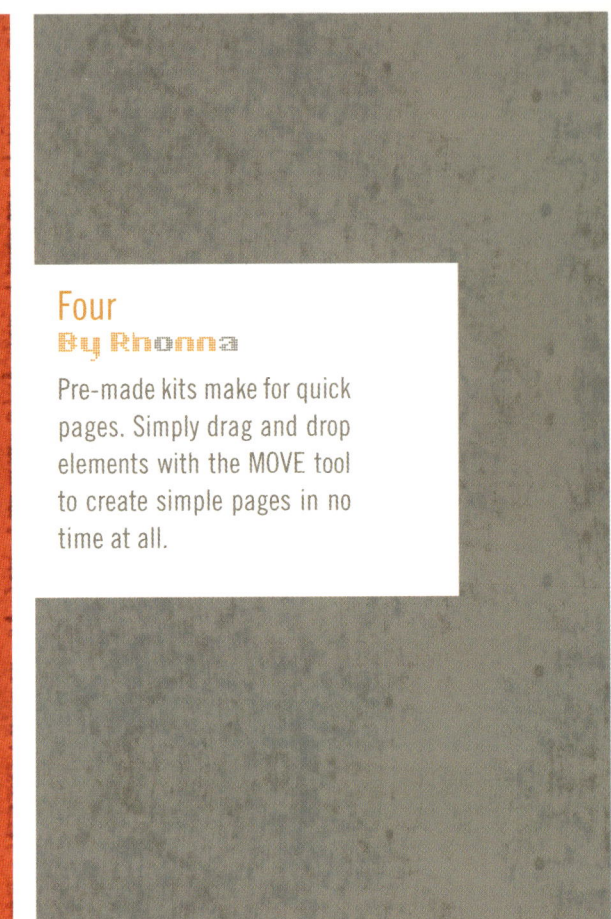

bailey sue at four

SEPTEMBER 14, 2004
A FEW DAYS AFTER DAD HURT HIS FINGER...
BAILEY: DAD, HOW'S YOUR FINGER COMING ALONG?
MOM: WHAT?
BAILEY: MOM, I ASKED DAD.

SEPTEMBER 15, 2004
MOM TOLD BAILEY THAT A. CHERIE HAD A BABY IN HER TUMMY.
BAILEY: AWWWWWW RIIIGHT MOM THAT'TH AWTHUMB! I WANT YOU TO HAVE A BROTHER OR SISTER IN YOUR TUMMY.

NOVEMBER 23, 2004
KNOWS HILLARY DUFF SONGS & SINGS THEM AT THE TOP OF HER LUNGS IN THE CAR. SHE CALLS HER HILLARY 'DUCK'.

DECEMBER 20, 2004
AT OLIVE GARDEN, BAILEY TOOK TOO LONG GETTING OUT OF THE BOOTH TO LEAVE.
MOM: WHAT IS TAKING YOU SO LONG, BAILEY?
BAILEY: MOMMY, I'M TRYING TO FIND YOUR PURTHE. YOU ARE A FORGETTY MOMMY & I ALWAYTH HAVE TO FIND YOU PURTHE. THANK GOODNESS FOR THE PRESENCE OF MIND OF THIS FOUR YEAR OLD!

Four
By Rhonna

Pre-made kits make for quick pages. Simply drag and drop elements with the MOVE tool to create simple pages in no time at all.

Confidence
By Rhonda

To create a basic layout, create cardstock papers, then add a photo, embellishments and a title.

CONFIDENCE

Jan '04

This photo of you has that sort of "okay bring it on" look that just exudes confidence. But looks can be deceiving, as you have such a tender heart. I hope during your journey you gain the confidence to face life with this look, but without hardening that heart of yours.

Pieces of My Heart
By Tina

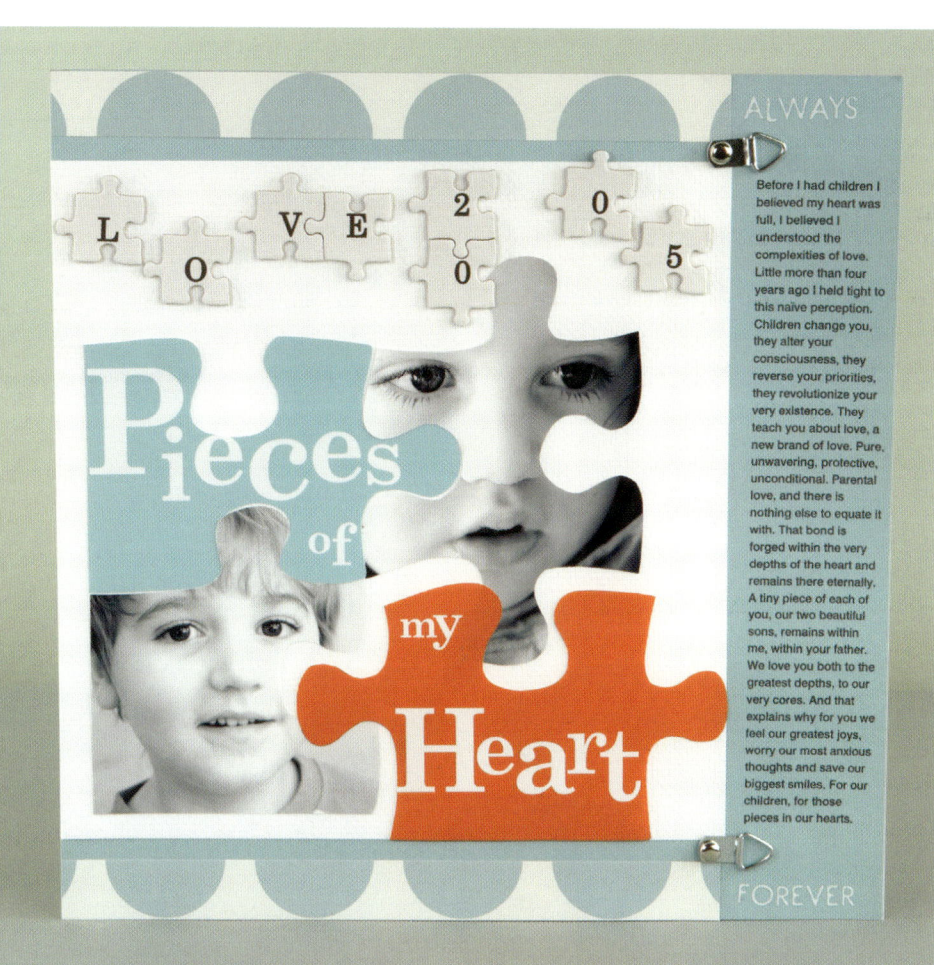

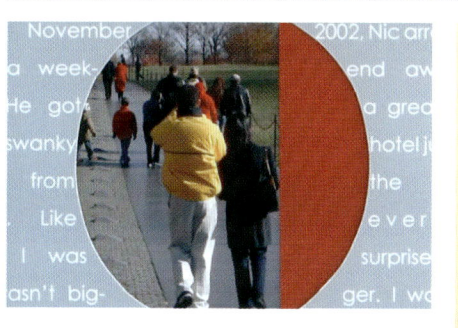

Print white text in a colored text box for a professional touch on a layout.

D.C.
By Traci

Make your text a visual element by using a word processing or page layout program to generate unique type.

CHAPTER TWO
TOOL BAR

It's a scrapbooker's dream: having every tool at her disposal without having to get up or even go to the store! As a digital artist, you will work with programs that include toolbars with tools you can access quickly. Think of this as your artist's kit. Just as you learned how to use scissors, crayons, paint and letters, you can learn how to use your program's tools to cut images, draw and add type. This chapter showcases common tools and how to use them in your layouts. You'll also see how some more advanced tools are put to work to repair photos, add a frame, draw a custom shape and more. Open your toolkit and start playing!

I found I could say things with color and shapes that I couldn't say any other way...things I had no words for.

—Georgia O'Keefe

NYC Skyline
By Lisa

To create special text effects, rotate text using the ROTATE tool.

02

IS IT ANY WONDER

you irresistible

THAT WE CAN'T RESIST

Irresistible You
By Rhonda

Select different parts of the layout and then cut out a piece of paper or embellishment. Use the MOVE tool to align and evenly distribute the page elements.

[see the things that matter most]
the {LITTLE} things

[see the things that matter most]
the {LITTLE} things

meditation

CON·CEN·TRA·TION

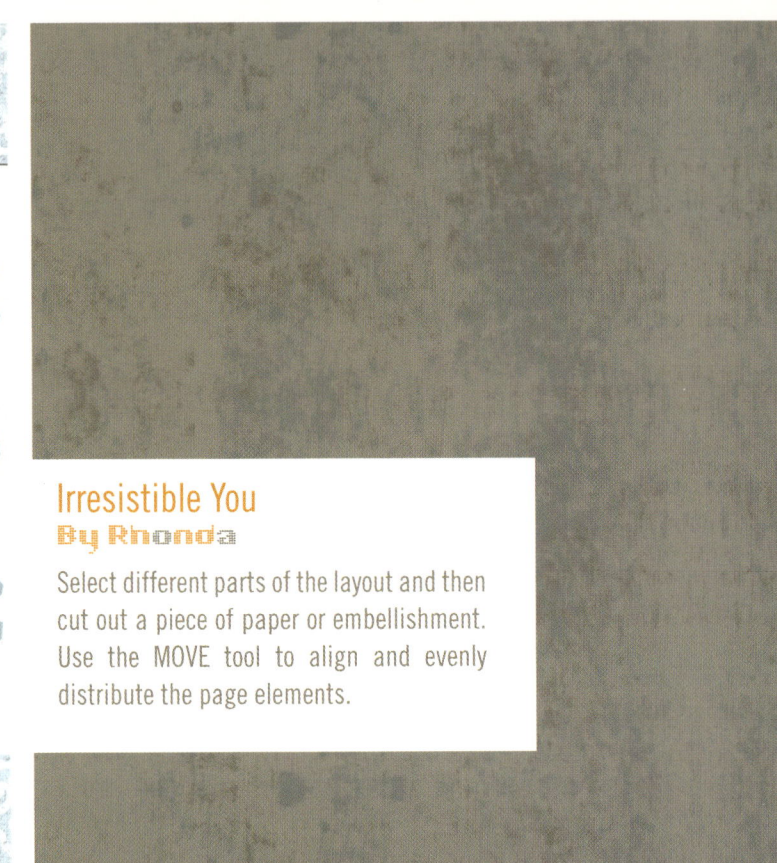

appreciation

Concentration
By Veronica

To draw basic shapes in your layout, use the MARQUEE tool.

I see my youngest child with a contagious smile. I see a happy 7 year old who enjoys playing with his friends. I see a first grader who loves school. I see a best friend to his older brother. I see an enthusiastic reader who adores his collection of Dr.Suess books. I see a compassionate soul who would do anything for you. I see a mischief maker who can't help but tell on himself. I see a son who is loved more than he will ever know. I see YOU -I see you.

photograph
is usually looked at - seldom looked into.

PHOTOGRAPHIC MEMORIES PHOTOGRAPHIC MEMORIES PHOTOGRAPHIC MEMORIES

Photograph
By Gina

Photo editing tools enable you to mimic special effects such as torn paper, Dymo labels and filmstrips.

Wakeboarding
By Laura

Cut out a precise image just like you would with a craft knife. In this example, Laura used the program's MAGNETIC LASSO tool to cut out the wakeboarder.

WAKEBOARDING

Living near the reservoir offers many opportunites for fun! During the summer, Gavin and his friends are a common sight on the water. Here Gavin was learning how to do flips with the wakeboard.

1

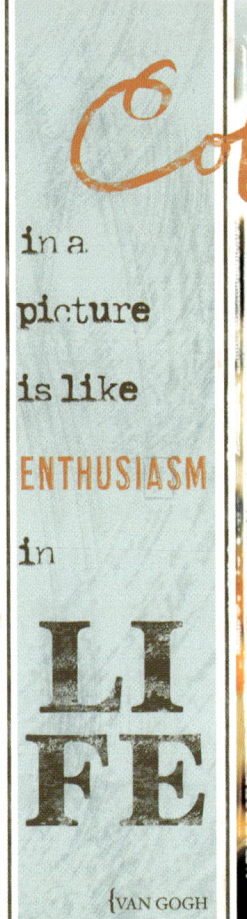

Color
By Rhonna

Emphasize your photos by adding dramatic edges. Here Rhonna used a special Photo Edge brush (included on the CD) as an ERASER tool to create the photo border.

Color in a picture is like ENTHUSIASM in LIFE

{VAN GOGH}

SEPT 2004

RE FRESH

It was a day of of swinging, sliding, running and rocking on the dinosaur at the park by Grandma Judy's house. You were on full speed until you fell in the woodchips and cut your hand. The injury put you in a sour mood and you were ready to leave, but a quick stop at the water fountain had you recharged, refreshed and ready for more. I was happy to see your spunk return!

Refresh
By Anne

If you want to match the color of your papers, text or embellishments to your photograph, try the DROPPER tool. You can build a custom color palette with this tool.

2 be Ella at Two
By Anna

To tint photos and add flair to your layout, use the GRADIENT and PAINT BUCKET tools.

Think
By Tina

In addition to alphanumeric characters, add special characters like the flower dingbat by using the TYPE tool. Tina went a step further and applied a special filter to the characters to create the look of emossed flowers.

My Favorite Place
By Jeri

Draw embellishments on the page with the PATH DRAWING tool. Also, alter your photographs by tilting them with the TRANSFORM tool or adding a frame with the FRAME tool.

Light
By Dena

Use the HEAL and CLONE tool to modify the background of photos.

Wedding Album
By Laura

To create a beautiful wedding album with pages like this, use the CROP tool to both size each photo to the height and width you choose as well as highlight the part of the photograph you want to emphasize.

CHAPTER THREE
CUSTOM BRUSHES

Angular, bright, fan and filbert. These are just a few of the brushes that a skilled artist might use to create a masterpiece. As a digital artist, you can have access to all these brushes and many more with the click of a mouse. You can paint, stamp, erase or add special effects with custom brushes made from feathers, fingerprints, doodles, textures or type. With brushes, you can tint a photograph, create custom paper, add a frame to a picture and more. Use the projects in this chapter to see just how versatile a brush can be.

Painting is just another way of keeping a diary.
—Picasso

Evidence. Little prints covering every surface. Proof of your exploration, your insatiable curiosity. If it exists, it must be touched, examined. Again, and again, just to ensure it has not changed. You rush around with an index finger extended whenever there is a button to be pushed. You leave a lasting impression, but not only with your fingertip. The fingerprints are just the physical evidence. Of your presence, of your impact, on our lives, and on our souls. Our baby, our son, you have changed our perspective. You have taught us, you have challenged us. In eighteen short months you have left an indelible imprint on our family of four. I look forward to watching that mark grow, extending beyond the walls of our home. Into the lives of others, into the world beyond.

The Myth of Fingerprints
By Tina

Scan a stamp of your fingerprint and create a one-of-a-kind brush to use on your layouts.

03

OLD NEWS

This should be old news to you but just in case you forgot:

We think you're an awesome kid.
We love your sense of humor.
We love your smile.
We love your quirks.
We are blessed by you.
We love you!

Old News
By Rhonda

Experiment with different objects to make custom brushes. Here Rhonda produced a custom brush from a scan of the Sunday newspaper and then used that brush to create the patterned paper.

SNOW

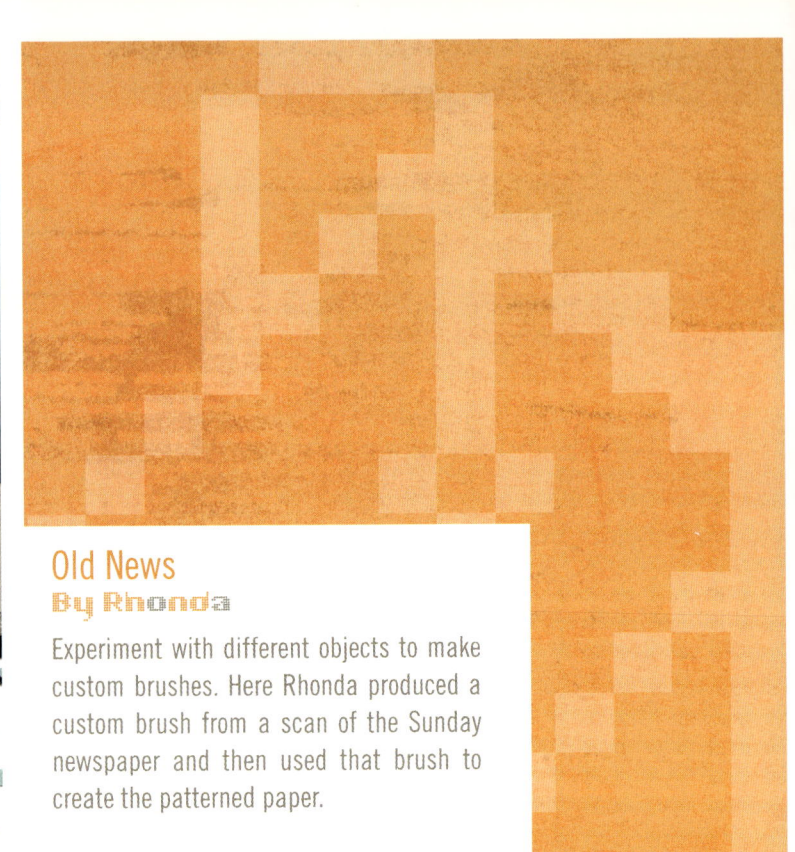

Jake,
I HOPE YOU WILL ALWAYS LOVE THE SNOW THE WAY YOU DID THIS DAY!
Mom

December 2001

Snow
By Laura

Photo-tinting brushes enable you to minimize distractions and emphasize the key part of a layout.

what must you think?

A BIG move, a NEW home & a BABY brother - We tried to PREPARE you for the months ahead but there was no telling how much you UNDERSTOOD. Your RESILIENCE to CHANGE has AMAZED us. We FEARED you might RESENT your new brother, but at first CURIOUS, you have fast become his PROTECTOR. What you THINK of all this will always remain a mystery, but what IS clear is how MUCH you ADORE this new little BEING in our LIVES - 01/2005

What Must You Think?
By Anna

Layer masks combined with custom brushes are useful for blending photos and making patterned papers.

October 8 2004
...an afternoon walk
golden sunshine
Autumn leaves
spending time with you

EXPLORING WALKING Destination

boy.

Boy
By Joanna

Crumpled saran wrap, feathers and other everyday household items work well for the basis for custom brushes.

Watching the Sunset
By Anne

Use brushes to stamp patterns and create custom paper. Change the size, rotation and color of the brush for variety.

watching the SUNSET

One of the best parts about our camping trip to Lime Kiln State Park was the gorgeous sunsets. Our campsite was just 100 yards from the beach, so every night after dinner we'd all walk down to the coast to find a spot on the rocks to watch the sun go down. The area is known for its heavy fog, but we were blessed with crystal clear skies every night which allowed us to see the full beauty of the sunset. Even Trevor was in awe and would sit motionless as he looked at the view (very rare, for sure). The sunsets alone were enough to make us want to return next year.

ANNUAL CAMPING TRIP – AUGUST 2004

LIME KILN STATE PARK

Chilling Out
By Veronica

In addition to the brushes included with your program, you can download pre-made brushes from internet sources.

If You Know
By Dena

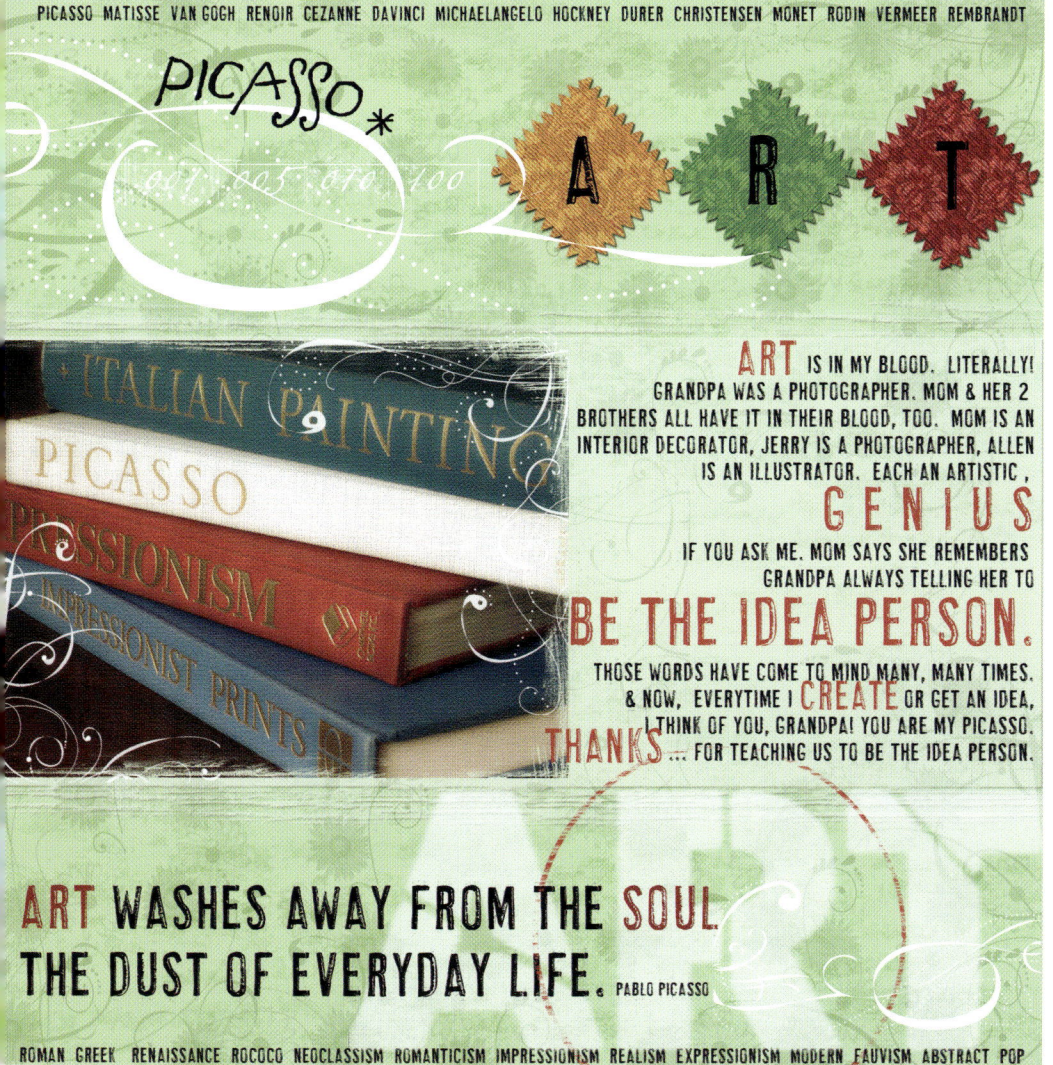

To add texture and age to a photograph, drag various brushes over a photo.

Art
By Rhonna

Design custom brushes by using photos of textures, scans of drawings, or art you create on your computer. In this layout, Rhonna made brushes from scans of concrete and peeling paint, drawings, and parts of a book.

Inside the Lines
By Gina

Create customized patterned paper with built-in brushes.

Happiness
By Rhonna

Any layout element can be enhanced with a brush. Try brushing the edges or corners of a layout, the borders of a photograph, a monogrammed letter or journaling.

Contact Cards
By Tracy

Add a hand-drawn image with a brush and create your own customized contact cards.

Suzanne
By Lisa

Use your own photography as inspiration and source for a custom brush.

That Look
By Rhonna

Text is another starting point for a brush. Here Rhonna built a brush from text ("that look") and then erased the background of the photograph with this custom brush.

whenyouget

that look

iknowyou'vebeen mischevious
but i love you just the same

::emptying the fireplace ashes all over your brother's head::dumping a 20 lb. bag of flour on the kitchen floor::

Brothers
By Veronica

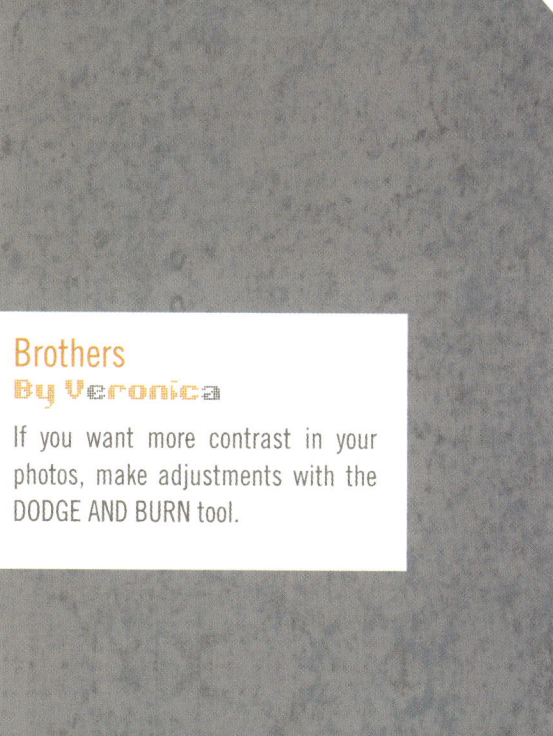

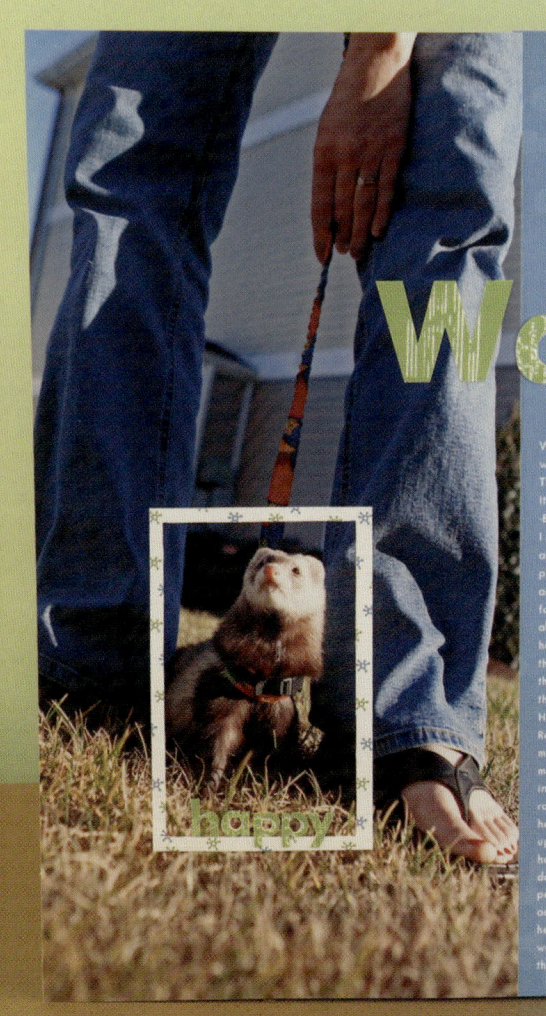

If you want more contrast in your photos, make adjustments with the DODGE AND BURN tool.

Walking with Butters
By Traci

Stamp characters such as dingbats to create custom frames and paper.

# CHAPTER FOUR
LIGHT MODES

Jenny Jerome Churchill quipped, "Treat your friends as you do your pictures and place them in their best light." Light is vital to a stellar photograph. And in digital scrapbooking, you can always guarantee your photos will be placed in their best light. Light modes can add a unique artistic look to your layouts and allow you to blend a photo, add an overlay, adjust the contrast or create other special effects. Check out how the artists in this chapter use light modes to enhance their layouts, placing them in their best light.

> There are painters who transform the sun into a yellow spot, but there are others who, thanks to their art and intelligence, transform a yellow spot into the sun.
>
> —Picasso

SHINE
beauty
play
PURE
SASSY
love

darling COUSINS

2 0 0 4

darling cousins darling friends

Cousins
By Rhonna

Vary the colors of your overlays until you get the desired effect. In this layout, Rhonna used OVERLAY LIGHT mode for the title, flowers and letter "B."

04

Sweetness
By Veronica

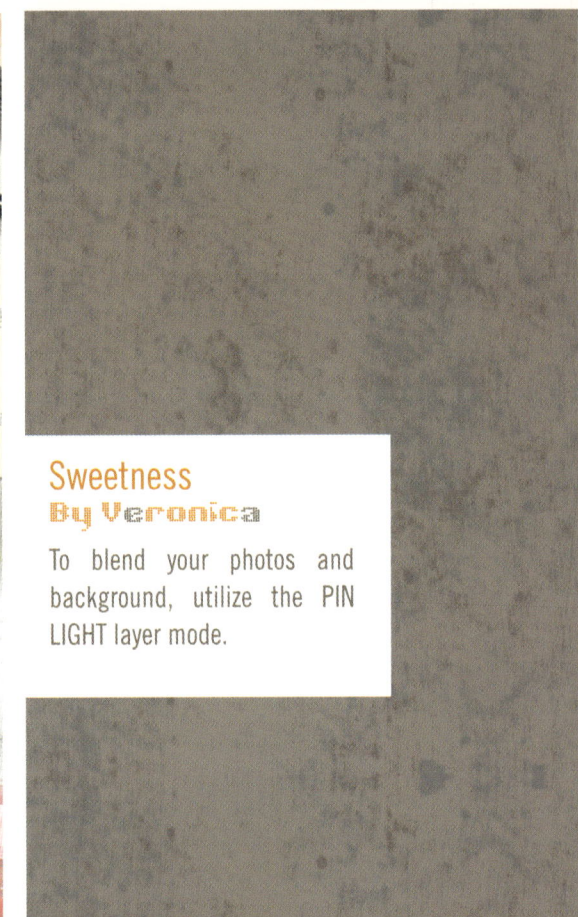

To blend your photos and background, utilize the PIN LIGHT layer mode.

- maybe she's born with it -

Focus
By Anna

Increase the contrast of photos with linear light.

focus on the things that you do Best
- Moms Advice, 09/04

Split Shift
By Traci

Create one image by merging photos taken during two different times. To emphasize the contrast in the two images, modify the light modes in each photograph.

Auto

t

n

splitshiftsplitshiftsplitshiftsplitshift

"We don't feel the need to be together all of the time." It's one of the funniest lines in Just Married, and a line Nic and I repeatedly quote. After the wedding, we had two months together before I spent three and a half months in Texas, then two weeks together before I spent a month and a half in Alabama. And all this after two years on separate coasts! When I got back from Alabama we were excited to settle down and finally be "a normal couple." Only that wasn't in the cards. My first job after getting back from Alabama was the squadron's swing shift supervisor. We were finally in the same state, only to be on dueling shifts! The good news is that it was only temporary. Tomorrow I go back to the day shift, and Nic and I will be one of those "normal couples" at last. I'm a little sad, though. There are things that I will miss. The best part of working opposite shifts was that we really truly valued the time we did have together. I'll miss Nic's lunches at home (I was usually still in my jammies), I'll I'll miss coming home for dinner. I'll miss sneaking in at night and trying not to be too loud (I was once "shushed" for unbuckling my belt). And most of all, I'll miss the mornings. My mornings started when Nic snuck back into bed after his shower, all warm and clean. Kissing me, poking me, generally bothering me. My kiss goodbye as he left for work and I snuggled back into the covers for 30 more minutes of sleep. I hope that even though we'll be spending more time together now, we'll value it just as much as our stolen moments on dueling shifts.

split shift

SPENDING THREE MONTHS ON OPPOSITE SHIFTS. TRACI 1400-2300. NIC 0730-1800.

Time Flies
By Rhonda
Use the SOFT LIGHT blend mode to create patterned paper from close-up photographs, such as photos of a clock used here.

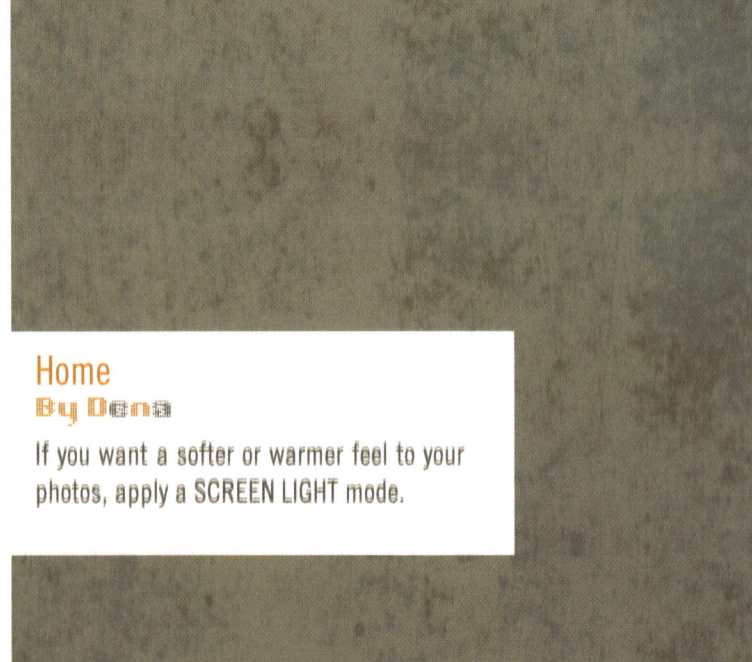

2004

How is it that in just one year you went from a 1-year old to a 3-year old? At the beginning of 2004 I still thought of you as my 1-year old, not a soon to be 2-year old. But at the beginning of this year I find myself thinking of you more as my soon to be 3-year old, not a 2-year old. Did time speed up here? Or am I finally facing the reality that I don't have a baby anymore?

2005

Home
By Dena
If you want a softer or warmer feel to your photos, apply a SCREEN LIGHT mode.

Unbelievable
By Rhonna

Some of the digital kits on the CD include patterned papers created using light modes.

Wish
By Gina

To touch up and repair photographs, use the DODGE AND BURN mode.

CHAPTER FIVE
FILTERS

Just like a filter separates what you want from what you don't want, filters in digital scrapbooking work the same way to create striking special effects. Depending on the filter used, such as dreamy, blur, color gradients or noise, you can filter part of a photo or layout to enhance the focal point and make a statement. Sift through this chapter and you'll fall in love with the artful pages you can create with filters.

To be truly creative, you have to work beyond what you know. Pushing the envelope is what being an artist is all about.

—John Ferrie

No more wondering where he gets it from, huh?

It's funny - every time we visit my parents, Aidan comes back with all these interesting little...um...TRICKS. Turns out that Poppy is taking advantage of those nights when Vic and I go out to teach Aidan everything in his repertoire of 'gross boy things.'

We had the raspberries when he was a baby, the push in your nose and make your tongue stick out, and the ever-popular 'make it look like your finger is all the way up your nose.' I have no doubt our next visit will result in some form of noises eminating from one's armpit.

Nana gets to spoil him, Poppy gets to teach him tricks. That's what grandparents are for, right?

MAY 2005

05

Tricks
By Lisa

Give photos an artsy look by using the Monday Morning (blue) filter.

39

Everything
By Veronica

To soften the skin tones in a photo, use the DIFFUSE GLOW filter.

Loving you changes *everything* for the better

[sienna · november 2004]

ME AT 3

JERILYN

1968

1968
By Jeri

Use one of the edge effects or frames in PhotoImpact to jazz up a photo.

'52
By Rhonna

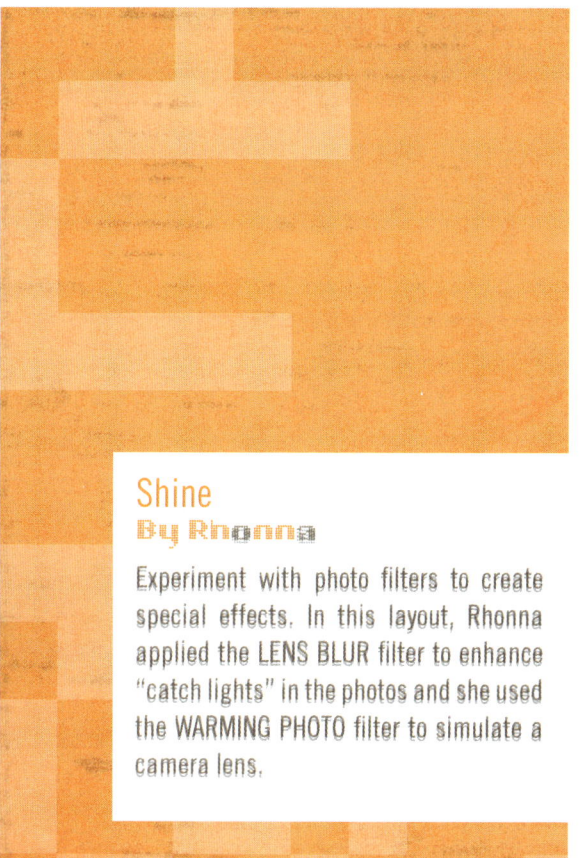

Explore the various filters available for your particular program. Here Rhonna applied a plug-in filter—Neat Image—to reduce the noise (graininess) of the photos.

Shine
By Rhonna

Experiment with photo filters to create special effects. In this layout, Rhonna applied the LENS BLUR filter to enhance "catch lights" in the photos and she used the WARMING PHOTO filter to simulate a camera lens.

The first moments...

blur

It all happened so fast! I wanted to enjoy the experience and intended to savor every moment of your birth. I was relaxed and excited at the prospect of finally meeting you. But then all of a sudden the contractions were coming so fast, the pain was more intense and it was as though my time had been snatched away from me. Within a short 20 minutes my smiles had turned to anguish and you arrived barely in one breath. There was no time for pain meds - The doctor barely arrived, but amongst it all I remember just a few of those moments: a glimpse of dark hair, the strength of your cry, and asking if you were indeed the little man we had so patiently been expecting.

The First Moments
By Anna
Use blur filters to add drama to a newborn photo.

1-17-05

art faces

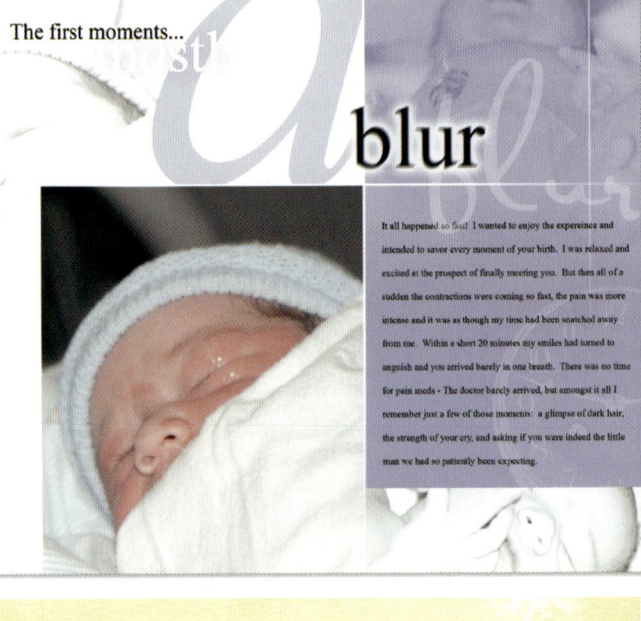

In one sitting •••••••••••••••••••••••••••••••••••• you bring your art to life!

Art Faces
By Rhonda
Use Photoshop plug-ins downloaded from the Internet to create unique effects on a series of photos.

Leaving DC
By Laura
Apply an AutoFX edge to photos, mats or backgrounds for an aged look.

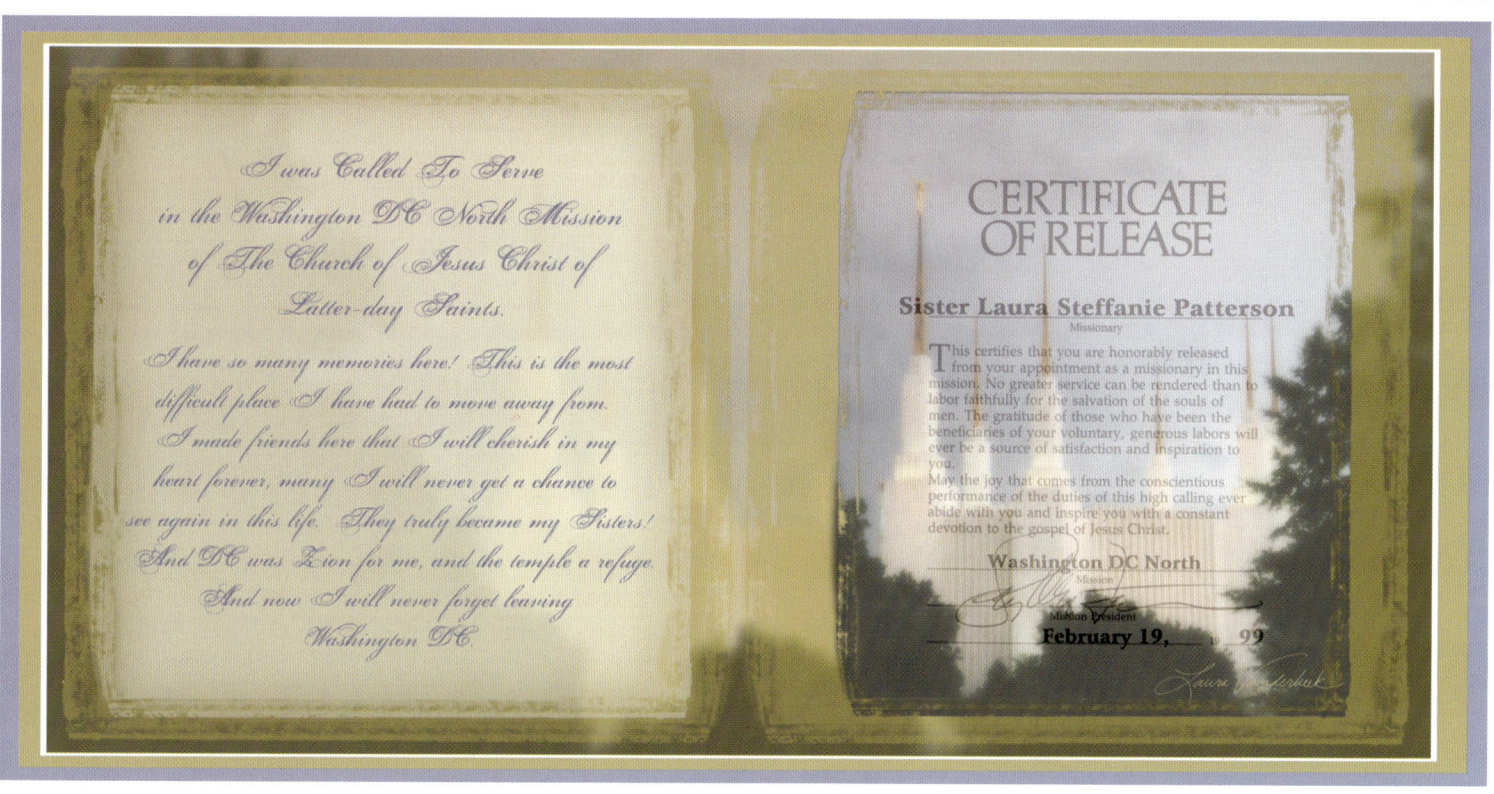

Hypnotized
By Dena
The NOISE filter will add texture to a photo or layout.

Spain
By Rhonna
For a dreamy and ethereal look, apply AutoFX's Dreamy filter.

jaya

Spain

{nineteen ninety nine age three}

EVERYDAY Princess

As the boys and I were looking through the photos we took during your party Peyton said, "Look -Lexi is a real princess! I didn't see her in that costume." I laughed and told him that there was no costume -all she did was put on the crown that was on her birthday cake. He giggled and said you belonged at Disneyland with the other princesses. You would never know from this photo that your hair was just braided back and you were wearing a cotton jogging suit. Yes, it's true. All that was needed to make you into the perfect little princess was the crown that topped off your birthday cake. But that is the beauty of of it -of you. You will learn as you grow up that you really won't need all the frills to make you special, to make you shine, to make you an everyday princess.

Everyday Princess
By Gina

Digital Image Pro's DIFFUSE filter can add a dream-like effect- perfect for a princess photo.

Incomparable
By Anne

Give sweet photos a soft, angelic look with the SOFT FOCUS filter in Paint Shop Pro.

INCOMPARABLE

Your sweet smile, nutty sense of humor, incredible memory, cute dimples, short fuse, desire to learn, and amazing beauty... There has never been, and will never be, anyone quite like you!

45

CHAPTER SIX
ELEMENTS

Imagine having all the embellishments you could dream of with just the click of a mouse: staples, brads, pebbles, flowers, tags, fibers, letters, glass, metal, paper (of course!) and more. That is one of the beauties of digital scrapbooking. Imagine being able to use the same embellishment over and over and over again. Your wallet will thank you! With digital layouts, you can scan a generic element, create it from scratch or use an element from a kit and incorporate it into your digital masterpieces. Read on to see how our artists created all kinds of fun, cool elements.

Art is not what you see, but what you make others see.

—Edgar Degas

Blessed
By Rhonna

Quickly create a digital layout by modifying pre-made kits. Simply re-color elements, cut them up, then use them to personalize a layout.

06

Happiness in family life is most likely to be achieved when founded upon the teachings of the Lord Jesus Christ.

family

47

3 in the Snow
By Rhonda
Design patterned paper using basic Photoshop tools and filters. If you are using printed paper along with your custom paper, you can adjust the colors so your paper matches the printed paper.

3 pairs of snow pants. 3 pairs of mittens.
3 pairs of boots. 3 hats. 3 winter coats.
1 warm winter day. 1 fresh snowfall. 1 hill.
3 sleds. 1 mom. 1 snowball fight.
1 snow angel. 1 snow ghost.
What does this add up to?
3 happy kids. 3 tired kids.
1 happy mom. 1 tired mom :)

Jan '05

3 in the snow

Temptation
By Veronica
Draw shapes and add texture to create your own custom digital papers.

Temptation
is a bare belly button just begging for a raspberry

9 months

Kennady

I am little but I already know there's no way my can resist this

MOM FACE

This Face
By Laura

Include digital tags by drawing and filling the tag and rounding the corners. Then add other embellishments such as eyelets, white strips, charms and ribbon.

BLESSED BEYOND *measure*

i really am the luckiest mom in the world...you have given me so much joy. you were born with a personality that is so magnetic. everyone loves to be around you. you are caring, kind, adorable & have a keen sense of style. you are also one of the funniest people i know...you were blessed with a spirit that is very content, very happy & very passionate. you have blessed our family so much... our family would not be the same without you... we need you. we love you.

natalia

cheers

serene

Family
By Rhonna

Mix and match different elements from several pre-made kits to increase your repertoire of layout possibilities.

Time of Your Life
By Gina

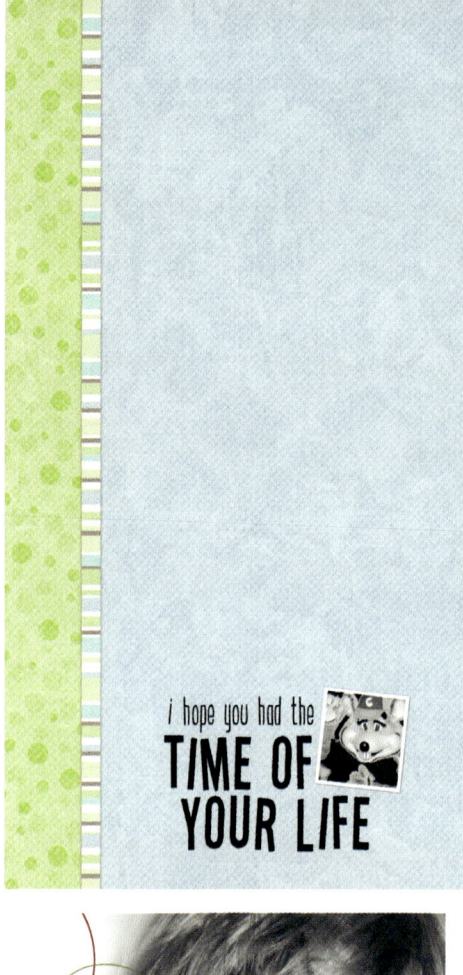

Make digital metal alphabet charms in Photoshop Elements and use them to jazz up a layout.

Christmas Aspnes Collection 2004
By Anna

Present a collection of family photos in your own digitally crafted postage stamps.

It crept up so quickly. Four, how can you suddenly be four years old? No longer a baby, or a toddler. Even preschooler is seemingly inappropriate. For now you are a boy. And you loudly proclaim it is so, a big boy at that. How could I disagree. Yet I marvel at the way you have changed especially quickly. I wonder at how I failed to notice the small changes, which resulted in one giant transformation. Into a child with a distinct personality, definite opinions, ideas and ideals. I'm proud of you, for finding yourself, for growing, for learning and even for changing. Today you are four. Rejoice and celebrate the individual that you are.

TODAY YOU ARE YOU! THAT IS TRUER THAN TRUE! THERE IS NO ONE ALIVE WHO YOU-ER THAN YOU! HAPPY BIRTHDAY

Wake Up! For Today Is Your Day Of All Days 02/01/05

FOUR

WILLIAM

Your Day of All Days
By Tina

Consider using a transparency as the first or underlying layer of a layout.

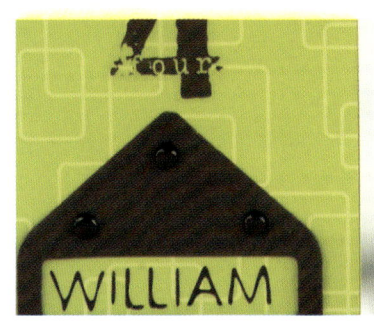

51

12
By Gina

Create realistic jewelry tags with the various shapes available in Digital Image Pro.

Somehow you turning twelve completely took me by surprise. You must be thinking I forgot how old you are but this is not the case. It is that time has passed by so quickly. You are my first born and this milestone birthday is the last year before you hit your teens. You are smart, considerate and a loving individual -a bit on the quiet side like myself who likes to read a good book and listen to your iPod. Your favorite band is Green Day and you have a great group of friends. You love to play basketball and also enjoy the challenge of complex computer games. You want to become a writer/illustrator when you grow up or a rock star. Today I see the handsome young man you are and also a glimpse of the wonderful man you will be. I love you.

zac
feb '05
age 12

Your love of lollipops started on Valentine's Day in 2004 when you first tried candy on a stick. You quickly ate that first lollipop and immediately asked for another. I know better than to keep them around the house, but if we have some because of a holiday or birthday party, you're always bugging me to give you one. It *is* cute how you do a little "happy dance" when I hand you the candy and you run off with a spring in your step. Once you start eating though, you get pretty serious and seem very calm and content. It's funny how something so simple and small can bring you so much happiness for a short time.

Lollipop love

Lollipop Love
By Anne

Stamping a pattern with a custom brush and using a striped pattern to fill the page are just two other methods for designing your own paper.

Nabuta Festival
By Anna

Embellish pages and create special layout elements with GLASS STYLES.

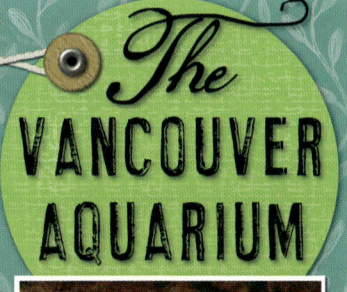

Vancouver Aquarium
By Jeri

With PhotoImpact's STAMP tool, you can design your own fibers and string to embellish any layout.

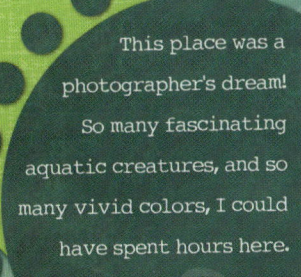

53

The Pumpkin and the Princess
By Anne

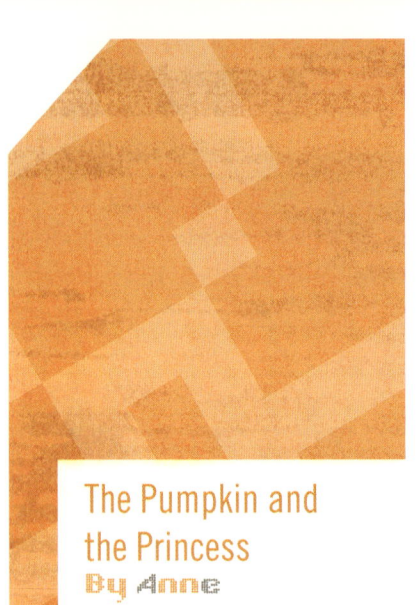

To add dimension, texture and shine to a layout, design and add metal tags or brads.

the pumpkin
and the princess

This Halloween you were pumped and excited for the holiday months in advance which gave Grandma Pat lots of time to make you a beautiful Sleeping Beauty costume. You couldn't wait to wear your one-of-a-kind costume to your school parade. You also couldn't wait to carve our pumpkin until you looked inside and freaked out when you saw the "guts" and seeds. Once I cleaned it out, you helped draw the face and supervised the carving. It was clear that you enjoyed the dress-up aspect of Halloween far more than the slimy pumpkin seeds

OCTOBER 2004 FIVE YEARS OLD

DETERMINATION

Jacob 2004

Determination
By Jeri

Experiment with pre-designed metallic elements already on your program, such as staples, eyelets, brads and metal-rimmed tags.

Though Jacob hasn't yet mastered swimming and still had to use the water wings this year, he's been getting more comfortable in the water.

OH
By Dena

Accent your layout by adding (unbreakable!) digital glass.

Let him stay little forever...

My Work
By Traci

Build a layout by adding layer over layer to the page. Here Traci printed a photograph onto a transparency and used it as one layer.

my work

This is not the job I thought I would have. Even two years ago, I never would have imagined that my job would be the business of F-15s. It's tough to put a finger on my exact job description. I'm the assistant commander of a 140 person flight. I manage the process of ensuring our aircraft are combat-ready. My flight makes sure that our pilots are given safe aircraft. I make sure that my flight is safe. Today I went to three meetings. I worked on reports. I yelled at a knuckle-head for not wearing protective equipment. I fell off a stand and landed on my butt in front of six of my troops. I watched the afternoon sorties launch. It's easy to get discouraged. To listen to the engines howl as a jet lumbers down the taxiway, to watch as they peel up and away from the runway, and feel like you don't contribute. To know that you could disappear and nothing would be better or worse for it. At those times you have to remember the small contributions. The change you made on someone's performance report to make it a tiny bit stronger, the accident you might have averted because you insisted that an airmen put on his goggles, the smile you offered to someone that was discouraged. I never feel quite as small, or quite as proud, as when I'm standing on the flightline. For better or worse, this is my job.

55

CHAPTER SEVEN
OVERLAYS

Everything's possible when creating a digital layout. You can still even create the look of a transparency by using an overlay, resulting in a multi-dimensional look. With digital layouts, you can create transparency effects from art, images, fonts, textures, color and other items. If you are creating a paper-based layout, print out your art on a transparency and attach the artwork. Or use your program's overlays to create the same effect in a digital layout. Find a favorite effect? Be sure to save it so you can use it in other layouts as well.

Art must be an expression of love or it is nothing.
—Marc Chagall

Always Aiden
By Nia
Overlap text in overlays, but change the font and font size for a cool, layered look.

07

Joy
By Anna

Design an overlay from simple shapes and images.

sisterhood

Laughter and tears, loving and fighting, playing and jealousy. All of these are part of your sisterhood. And over the past three years I have seen you two truly become sisters. I have seen the jealousy over my attention, the fighting over the toys, and the tears over the littlest things. But I have also seen the laughter you share, and the loving nature towards each other. And these are the moments that will bind you together as sisters.

Sisterhood
By Rhonda

With custom brushes and the ERASER tool, recreate the look of a transparency made with the packing tape transfer technique.

snow fun

winter sledding delight

There is nothing like sledding at Grandma and Grandpa Vanderbeek's house. You simply walk into the backyard and hop on your sled. And the best part is that all you have to do to get back to the top is wait for the snowmobile to pick you up. You can find a spot on the seat of the snowmobile or you can ride your tube while holding onto the back of the sled or tow rope. Today we went from 9:30am until 2:30pm and then ate and took a break. We were back out at 4:00pm until dark. This was a full day of amazing fun!

playground

laughter

snowmobiling

sledding

family-fun

Snow Fun
By Laura

Consider using an overlay to frame photographs in a digital layout. You can also print the overlay on a transparency if you want to use the overlay frame in a paper-based layout.

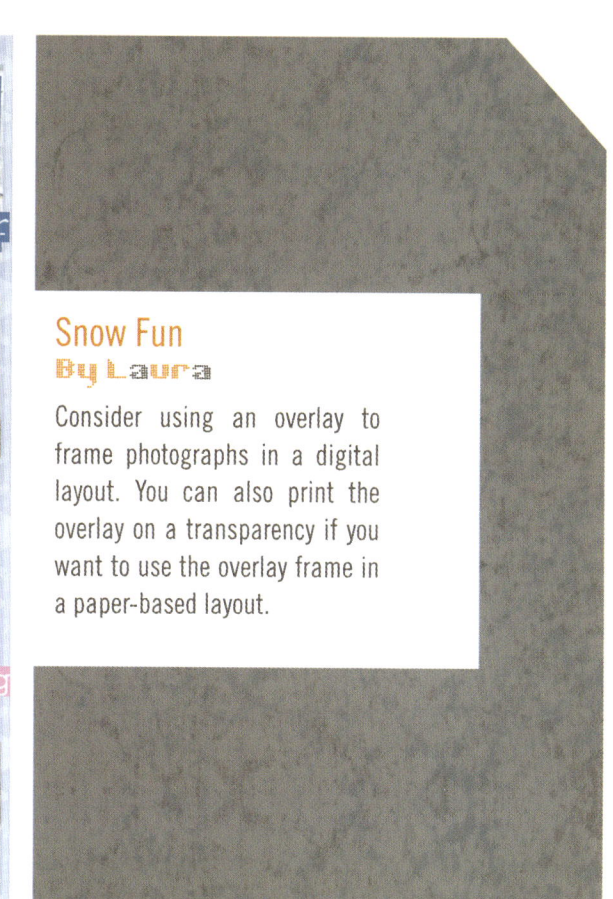

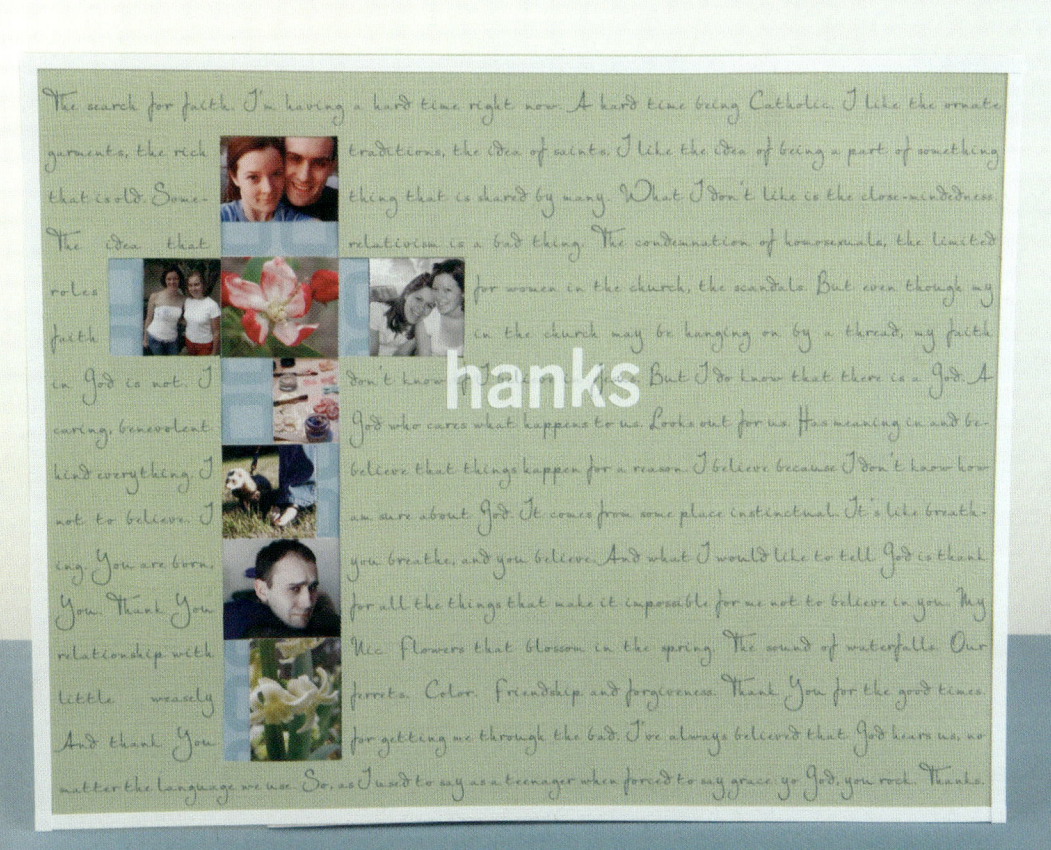

hanks

Thanks
By Traci

Build an image by using simple shapes (here a cross made from two rectangles) and then use that image as an overlay.

Amanda
By Veronica

Change layer modes with text overlays to make stunning effects on your pages.

The Good Stuff
By Gina

Custom text overlays are another way to incorporate overlays on a layout.

- big hugs
- pinchable cheeks
- baby hair
- sweet smile
- big brown eyes
- scrumptious nose
- Peyton kisses
- holding my hand
- charming personality
- delightful laugh
- the love you give
- that's the good stuff

December 2003

Carefree
By Anne

Create an overlay using a floral image such as the spray of flowers on the top layer of this layout.

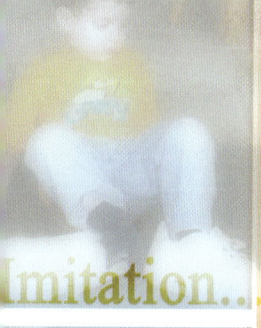

care free

When Dad decided to work on the sprinklers while you were playing in the backyard, you were treated to an unexpected shower. Rather than running for cover & moving off the grass, you stayed right in the middle of the water. You had a great time dancing in the water and you didn't seem to care that your clothes were soaking wet. Your spontaneous nature definitely won out over being sensible, but I think that's a good thing every once in a while!

SEPTEMBER 2004

Footsteps
By Dena

Text overlays are a simple way to add text and maximize space.

Imitation...

They say that it is the sincerest form of flattery. And if that is true.... Daddy should be VERY flattered! You are always looking for ways to imitate him whether it be in copying his comic routines or dressing like him or wearing his shoes. I have to wonder.......

Will you follow in Daddy's Footsteps

Imitation is the sincerest form of flattery......Imitation is the sincerest form of flattery......Imitation is the sincerest form of flattery......

Reflect
By Rhonna

Try different fonts for text, overlaying photos, elements or the entire layout.

{beingachild

enjoylife

california summer two thousand four

Enjoy
By Joanna

When you build your layers, enhance the consistency of the layout by echoing design elements from layer to layer (such as the snowflakes in this layout).

Infatuation
By Tina

As you work with text overlays, try varying the transparency, color and placement of the overlays.

The Real You
By Veronica

If you often include an overlay in your layouts, save time by creating and using a template.

So many people never get the chance to meet
the real you
they waste their time saying things like,
"Oh I'll bet she's a handful!"
And what they never get to see is what I get to see...
everyday
I get to see your softness.
I get to hear the little rasp in your voice
when you tell me you love me.
I get to feel those tiny arms and legs
wrap tightly around me when you don't want me to let go.
I get to feel more kisses in one day
than most people experience in a lifetime.
But most of all...
I get to be
loved by you!
And that is the most
REAL thing about you!

THERE IS NOTHING QUITE LIKE THE DAWN OF A BEAUTIFUL NEW DAY, THE CRUNCH OF FALLEN LEAVES BENEATH MY FEET, AND A BREATH OF CRISP AUTUMN AIR!

COLORFUL LEAVES AND CRISP AUTUMN AIR

Sherwood Hills Golf Course — *September 29, 2004*

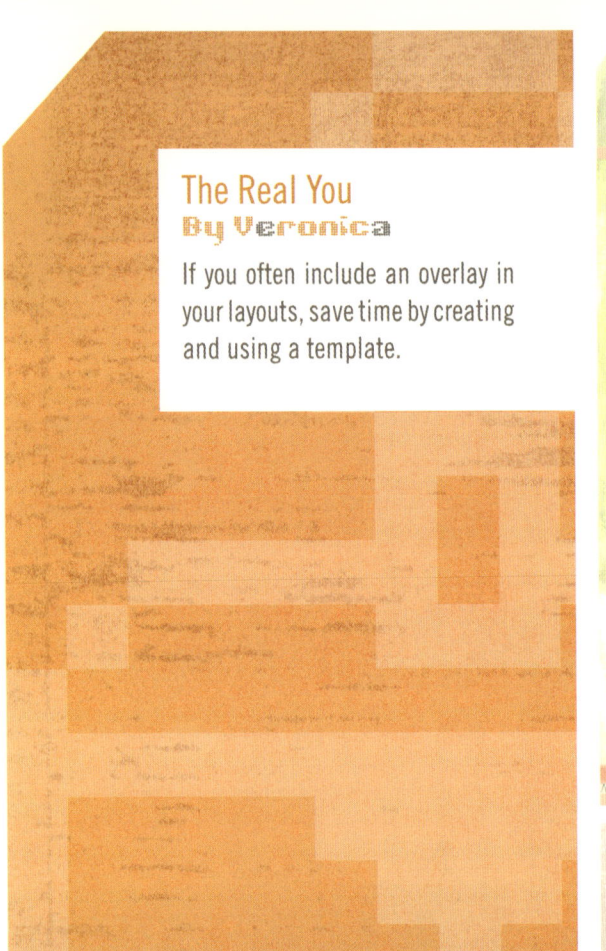

Autumn Golf
By Laura

To add emphasis to the text overlay and to differentiate it from a busy image, include a sheer block of color between the photo and the text. Consider using light colors for the background and bold colors for the text.

A Boy and His Ball
By Lisa

Print text in a circle or other shapes. For page-based designs, print the overlays on transparencies, trim, then attach.

You at Age Four
By Rhonna

Use photos as one type of overlay.

CHAPTER EIGHT
GALLERY

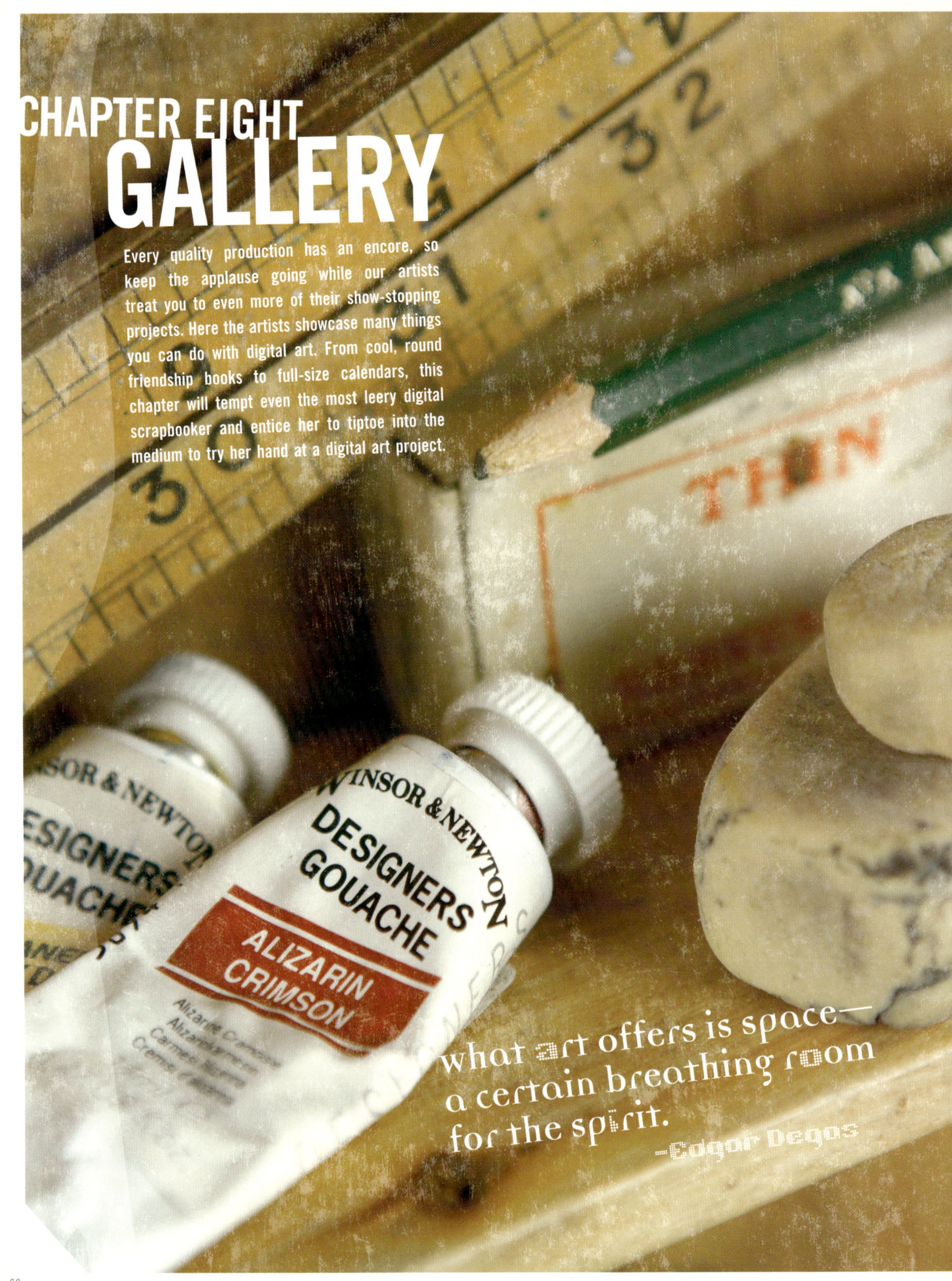

Every quality production has an encore, so keep the applause going while our artists treat you to even more of their show-stopping projects. Here the artists showcase many things you can do with digital art. From cool, round friendship books to full-size calendars, this chapter will tempt even the most leery digital scrapbooker and entice her to tiptoe into the medium to try her hand at a digital art project.

*what art offers is space—
a certain breathing room
for the spirit.*
—Edgar Degas

LAX
By Tracy

With different frame styles, you can echo colors or pick a frame style that suits the mood of your layout. Here Tracy used an artistic colored pencil filter to showcase the photos in this layout.

08

Color
By Rhonda

Create your title by cutting it from a portion of a photo.

Go Speed Racer
By Gina

Watermarks are one way to customize your background papers and photos.

She is beautiful. She is a woman.
Shakespeare

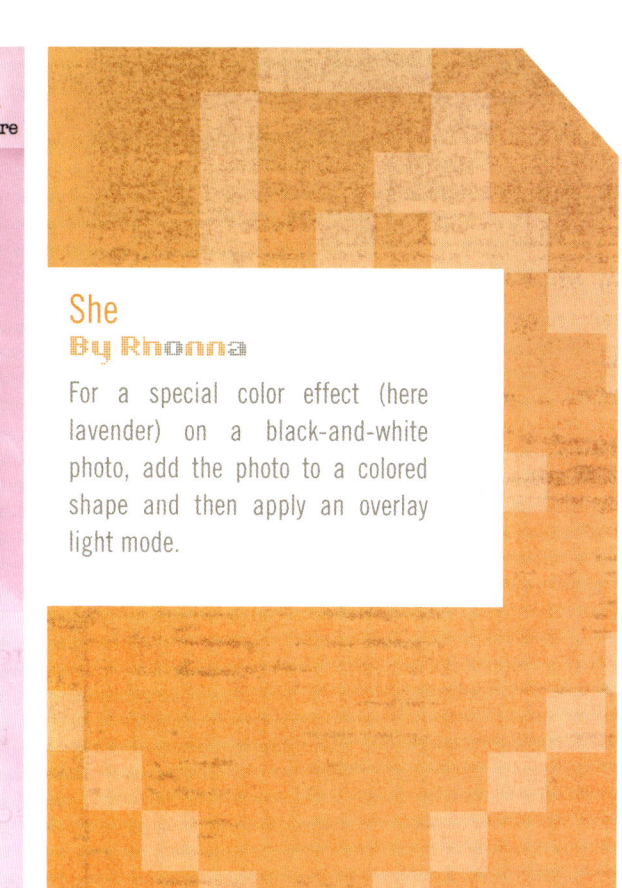

velda lindsay born in heber city, utah in the home of her grandmother father: john allen lindsay; mother: ella bunnel lindsay; birthday june 24, 1913 two week later she & her mother returned to their home where she was raised with 3 older sisters, 1 younger sister & two younger brothers. ella died when velda was 18. this was devastating to all, but especially velda.

She
By Rhonna

For a special color effect (here lavender) on a black-and-white photo, add the photo to a colored shape and then apply an overlay light mode.

Mini Calendar
By Joanna

Create a mini calendar with family photos. Print the days on the photograph and use rub-ons for the months. Trim and place in an acrylic holder.

Big Wide World
By Anna

Add text on a curved path for distinct text placement.

I am so excited about the adventure on which you have already embarked. As you make this momentous journey, remember always to have confidence in yourself. Always trust your instincts and follow your heart as you find your way in this world. Never be afraid to step out to fulfill your own happiness and reach for your dreams and so many opportunities just lying within your grasp. There is so much ahead of you to experience and

there is a big wide world out there just waiting for you to make your mark.....

30 minutes is all it takes to drive to Mount Baldy...

but from the top of the mountain, it feels like another world!

OCTOBER 2004

30 Minutes
By Anne

With your program's SHAPE tools, round corners and draw curves.

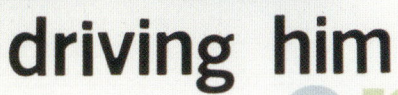

Driving Him Crazy
By Traci

Start with a scanned image to design a customized brush. Then use your custom brush as a stamp on parts of your layout.

Standing Out in the Crowd
By Nia

Build a unique background by creating, copying and layering the same text.

Très Chic
By Rhonna

The best way to learn your program's features is to experiment. Have fun with photo edges, metal elements, fabric tags, vellum, stitching, brushes and papers. You can also get a quick start by using pre-made kits such as the templates on the CD (including one for this layout).

Holiday Cards
By Veronica

NOEL: Convert your photos to grayscale and adjust the brightness, matching the colors and brightness as much as possible. If necessary, use the DODGE/BURN tool to darken or lighten any photo areas that need fine tuning.

SNOWMAN: Scan a drawing and then enhance it by adding shapes, text or borders.

Circle of Friends Mini Book
By Dena

Base your design and book layout on a fun shape such as a circle used for this book about friends.

The Girl with Kaleidoscope Eyes
By Tina

Most photo editing programs include several special effects for modifying photos. Here Tina added the kaleidoscope effect to pictures of flowers; she cropped the kaleidoscope images to a starburst shape and pasted them into circles.

"Honey Do" List
By Traci

Design your own customized to do list using text and images. Be sure to include enough blank space to write your list!

Ice Cream Sundae
By Lisa

To create patterned paper, draw stripes, circles and other shapes with your program's SHAPE tools. Fill the shapes with colors or patterns and add borders or outlines.

Calendar
By Laura

Create a large hanging calendar with your photos. Select your favorite photographs so you can enjoy them all year long.

75

CHAPTER 8 SCANNING & RESTORATION TIPS & INFORMATION

Siblings
By Veronica

Consider other sources than your digital camera or scanner for pictures. If you have a video camera, capture and use images from this digital media in your layouts. Even though you get only low-resolution images, you can use brushes and filters to make the photo work.

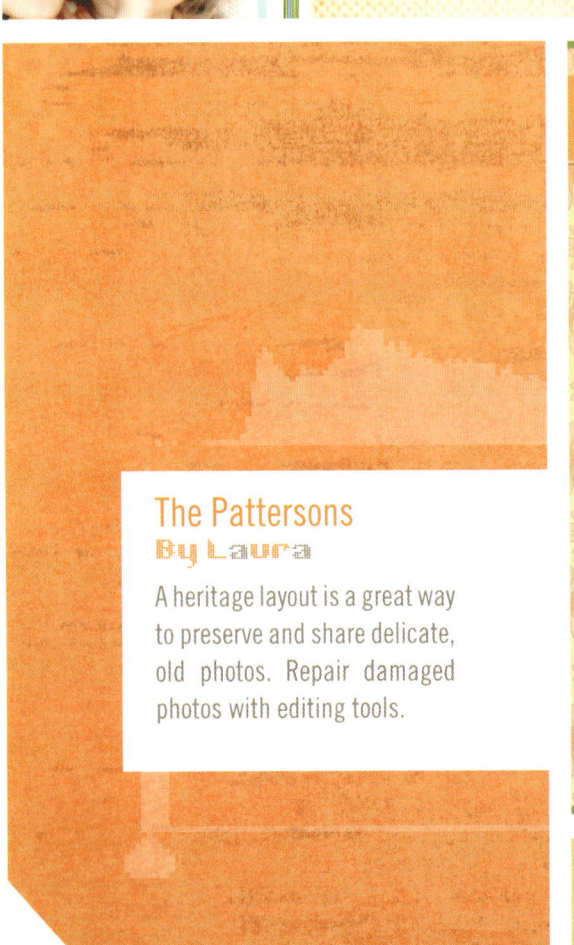

The Pattersons
By Laura

A heritage layout is a great way to preserve and share delicate, old photos. Repair damaged photos with editing tools.

76

Serendipity
By Anna

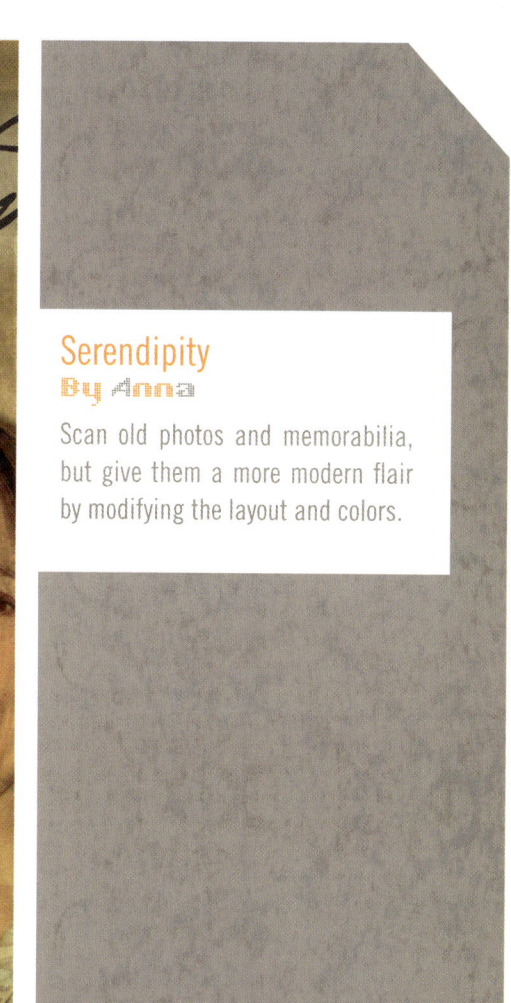

Scan old photos and memorabilia, but give them a more modern flair by modifying the layout and colors.

Poet
By Nia

Update a photograph by scanning it and then modifying its colors.

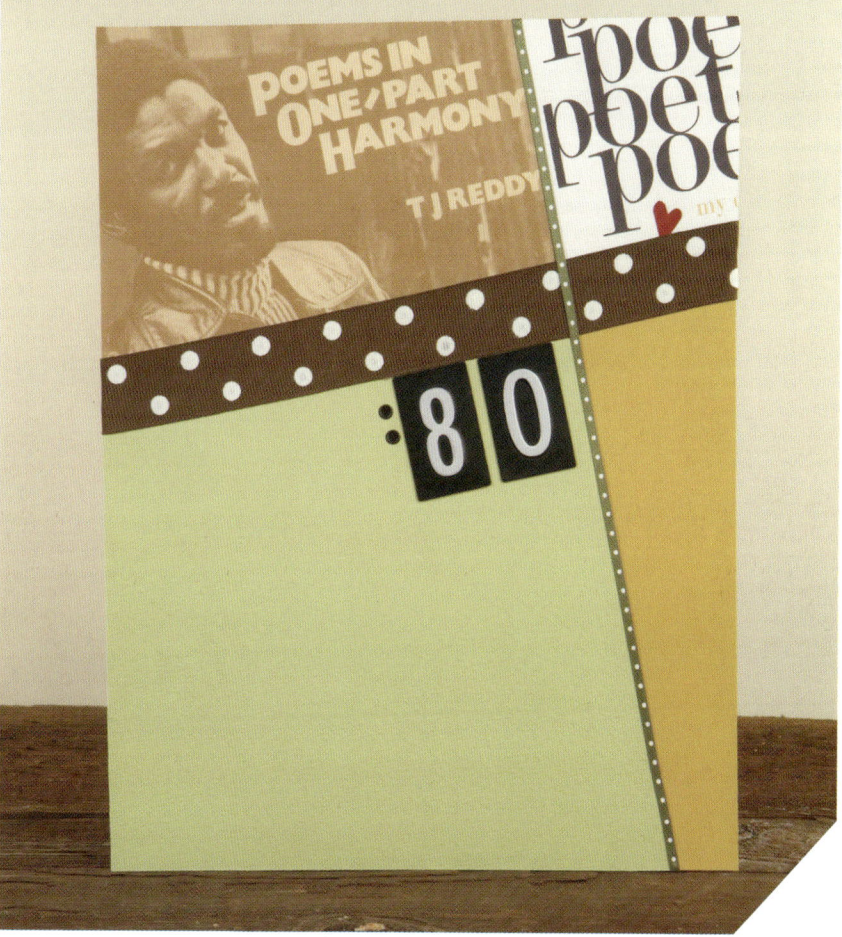

77

Magic
By Rhonna

For a quick layout, use digital kits. Several designs are provided on this book's CD, including one for this layout.

jaya age eight

you are the kind of girl who makes everyone around you feel good about themselves ... that is not an easy thing to do...I see it as pure magic.

m
magic

a happy heart makes the face cheerful. PROVERBS 15:13

This couldn't be more true of you Erin. When you are happy your whole face lights up. I especially love it when your little tongue comes peeking out, a sure sign of your happy heart!

February 2005

your heart peeks out

Heart
By Rhonda

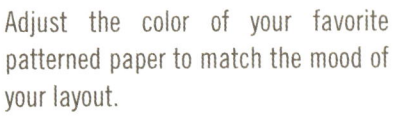

Adjust the color of your favorite patterned paper to match the mood of your layout.

CHAPTER 8 DESIGNING WITH DIGITAL KIT

The kit used in all of these layouts is on the included CD.

The Art of Life
By Gina

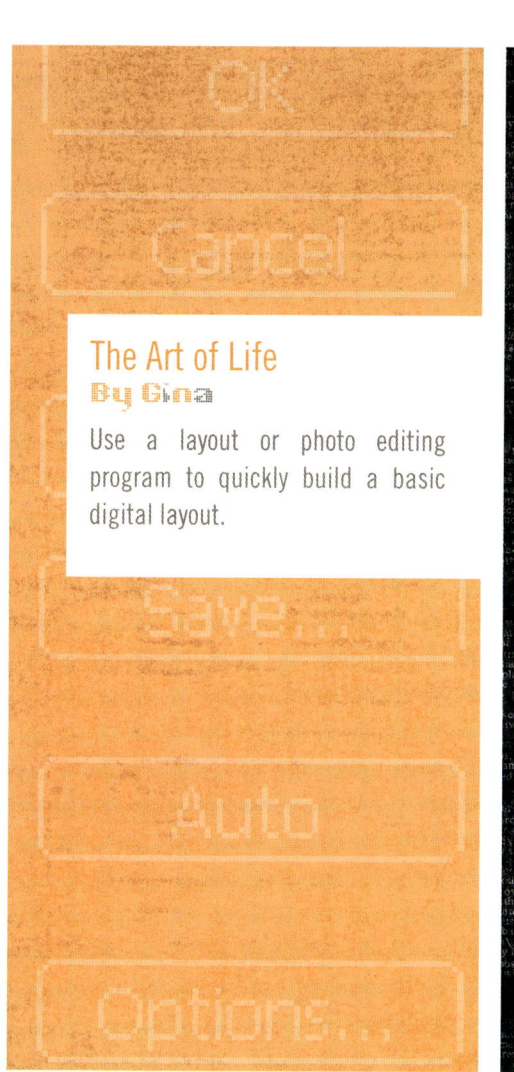

Use a layout or photo editing program to quickly build a basic digital layout.

Cutie Pie
By Nia

Use editing tools to match the palette for your digital page to the colors in printed paper.

INDEX 01: HOW TO'S & CREDITS

CHAPTER ONE

Road Trip
SOFTWARE: PS
FONT: Gill Sans
INK: 7 Gypsies walnut ink
PAPER: Rusty Pickle, Daisy D's
SIGNAGE: MM

Add drop-shadow to text: Add text directly to the photo, using layers. Apply a brown drop shadow to the title and subtitles. To add a drop shadow to text, create a new text layer using the **TYPE** tool. Type the text and then select all of the text. Click **LAYER >> LAYER STYLE >> DROP SHADOW** and adjust settings as desired.

Living
SOFTWARE: PSE
FONT: Interstate
PAPERS: AL, Paper Source, FiberMark
RUB-ONS: AL

Crop and move photos to create a collage: Create a new page that is sized 8"x12" and set to 300 dpi. Open the photos that you want to use for the collage. Crop the photo using the **CROP** tool and adjust the size as needed. (Note: It's important that the cropped photo and page are set to the same resolution.) Using the **MOVE** tool, move each photo over to the new page by dragging and dropping. Position exactly where you want. Using the **TEXT** tool, draw an outline in the area that you want the text to be. Select the text color, size and font. Then type the text. (Here Tracy selected a color from one of the photos for the text so that they coordinate.)

Storm
SOFTWARE: PS
FONTS: Virginia Plain, Dartangnon ITC, Donaldson Hand

Create a custom beveled slide mount: On a new layer with transparent background, draw a shape using the **ROUNDED RECTANGLE** tool. Create a cut out from the rectangle using the **SUBTRACT FROM SHAPE AREA** tool. Open the background you want to use for the slide mount; you can use any images you have available on your computer. Click **EDIT >> DEFINE PATTERN** to create your new pattern. Then fill your slide mount with your new pattern. To do so, click **EDIT >> FILL**. In the dialog box that appears, choose the Pattern option and click on the Custom Pattern drop-down list box to find your new pattern (it is usually the very last one). Then click OK. To add depth to the mount (making it look beveled), click on the Layer Style tab and then click the drop-down list box and choose Bevels.

Taylor
SOFTWARE: PSP
FONTS: AL Postmaster, AL Professor, Teletype

Add drop-shadow to paper: On a new layer with a transparent background, draw the shape of the paper piece. (Use the **SELECTION** tool and select Rectangle as the shape type.) Fill the shape with color at 100% opacity using the **FLOOD FILL** tool. Use the **PAINT BRUSH** tool with a custom brush to stamp on pattern. Apply the drop shadow by selecting **EFFECTS >> 3D EFFECTS >> DROP SHADOW**.

Reality Check
SOFTWARE: PS
FONTS: GeosansLight, Century Gothic, Miss

Create a new layer: Keeping all objects in separate layers is the best way to work in Photoshop. By using layers, you can add separate filters and effects to each item without affecting the other. You can create as many layers as needed. Click **WINDOWS >> LAYERS** to display the Layers palette. To add a new layer, click the **CREATE A NEW LAYER** button or use the **LAYER >> NEW >> LAYER** command.

Magnifico Mexico
SOFTWARE: PS
FONT: AL Old Remington

Add an outline to a shape: Select the **SHAPE** tool to draw the shape you want to outline. Then draw the shape. Use the Stroke feature to add the outline or border to the shape. For this example, Rhonna drew circle borders with the **ELLIPITCAL** tool. (Hold down the Shift key while drawing the shape to create a perfect circle.) Also, she used her custom grunge brushes to erase parts of the border.

Better Things
FONTS: PR8 Charade, Interstate
PAPER: Paper Fever
SNAPS: MM

Create text effects: Create a large **TEXT BOX** and type text in a point size that fills the space. Set the fill color to blue and the text color to white. You can then print, trim, round the corners and attach this text box as well as the photos to a scrapbook sized piece of cardstock. For the journaling, create a text box with a beige fill. Type the letter 'A' in a point size that fills the space, and set the text color to a darker shade of the same beige. Create another text box with no fill and then type text for this text box. Layer this second text box over the first. You can print, trim and adhere these text boxes.

Ocean
SOFTWARE: PS
FONTS: AL Singsong, AL Old Royal

Add a stroke to paper and photos: On photo or paper layer, display the Layers palette and open the Blending Options menu. Choose **STROKE**. In the dialog box that appears, choose the size, position, blend mode, opacity, fill type and color of your stroke. For position, choose Inside to give your square or rectangular objects squared corners. For rounded corners, choose Outside. Center is great for text. Click **OK** after you have made your selections.

Four
SOFTWARE: PS
FONT: AL Uncle Charles
KIT: "Forever Kit" by Rhonna Farrer (included on CD)

Customize a kit by moving the elements around: Open your patterned paper from your kit. On a new image with a transparent background, drag and drop it onto your new page, by using your **MOVE** tool. Open up each of the elements you want to use. Drag and drop them onto your layout. Add a drop shadow and text.

Confidence
SOFTWARE: PSE
FONTS: AL Highlight, AL Messenger

Create papers and text: Create the cardstock papers using the **RECTANGLE** tool. Create the transparency using the **RECTANGLE** tool and then adjusting the opacity. Add the photo and elements by dragging and dropping them using the **MOVE** tool. Add the title and journaling by using the **TYPE** tool. To rotate the text box, use the **MOVE** tool. Add the stamp by using the **TYPE** tool and then the **ERASER** tool to mimic the look of a stamp.

Pieces of My Heart
FONTS: Century Schoolbook, Halvett Medium
PAPER: American Crafts
PUZZLE LETTERS: Li'l Davis
BRADS: MM
RUB-ONS: AL

Create white text on a colored background and puzzle shapes: Create a **TEXT BOX** and then fill with background color. Set text color to white and type in title. (Here the text is positioned so when the puzzle pieces are cut, the text fits inside.) To create the puzzle shapes, scan pieces of an actual puzzle. Enlarge and then cut out templates for the puzzle pieces. (This method ensures the puzzle shapes suits the photos.) Trace the templates directly onto the photos and title blocks, cut out and position on page.

DC
SOFTWARE: ID
FONT: Century Gothic
PAPER: Anna Griffin

Create letters filled with text: Create a background of cardstock, patterned paper and photos. In the software program, type the letter "D" and then select a size, font and color. Select the letter and then use the **TYPE >> CREATE OUTLINES** command. Type the text you want to use to fill the letter. Select the text, copy and paste it to the outline shape. Follow the same procedure to create the letter "C". Print the letters on glossy paper. Then cut out and adhere to layout.

CHAPTER TWO

NYC Skyline
SOFTWARE: ID
FONTS: Imperator Bronze, Placard Condensed, Middle Ages, Phlax, Marcelle Script, Serifa bt
INK: Colorbox/Clearsnap
BRADS: Two Peas in a Bucket

Create background text: Create a full-page text block of background text, setting the font color to light gray or 20% black. Crop and arrange photos, but do not adhere. Using a graphics or word processing program, add large text blocks over the background text. Use the **ROTATE** tool to vertically align two of the text blocks. Print, crop ½" off all four sides, and round corners. Mat and adhere photos, and lightly ink the outside edges.

Irresistible You
SOFTWARE: PS
FONTS: Hannibal Lecter, Hootie!

Cut and copy papers and elements: Scan generic elements you want to include in your digital layout. Using the **MARQUEE** tool, cut the paper pieces you want to use from the scan(s) and paste them into your digital layout. Drag and drop the negative strip and cut a section using the **MARQUEE** tool; include the cut piece in your layout. Do the same for the brad and other elements. Create duplicate layers and then use the **MOVE** tool to evenly align and distribute the page elements in the layout.

ABBREVIATIONS

AL: Autumn Leaves
MM: Making Memories
CI: Creative Imaginations
PS: Adobe Photoshop
PSE: Adobe Photoshop Elements
ID: Adobe InDesign
PSP: JASC Paint Shop Pro
DIP: Microsoft Digital Image Pro
PI: ULEAD Photo Impact

Concentration
SOFTWARE: PS
FONTS: AL Landscape, Goudy Old Style, Futura Lt BT, AL Oxygen, AL Verdigris, AL Highlight
Draw basic shapes: Delete part of your photograph by selecting the photo layer, selecting the **MARQUEE** tool (**SINGLE ROW/COLUMN**), and pressing the Delete key. To draw with the **MARQUEE** tool, click the tool, select the shape, and drag in the layout area to draw the shape. (TIP: Hold down the Shift key to draw a square or circle.) To fill the shape with color, use the **EDIT >> FILL** command. Use a custom brush to erase parts of the shape.

Photograph
SOFTWARE: DIP
FONTS: Harting, Voluta Script, Plastique, Beer Dip
Create torn paper, Dymo labels and filmstrips: For the torn paper, open a piece of background paper and then draw a jagged line around all sides of the paper using the **FREEHAND** tool. Invert the selection and then press the Delete key. If you want to add a shadow, click the **EFFECTS >> SHADOW** command, choose from any of the preset shadows, and click **DONE**. For the Dymo labels, insert a square with the **INSERT >> SHAPE** command. Change the shape so that the square is a long rectangle. Using the **PAINT BUCKET** tool, fill the rectangle with color. Click the **TEXT** tool and choose the font, size and color for the text. Type the text for the Dymo label. For the filmstrip, create the first box by inserting a square and modifying the shape and placement so that it is a rectangle placed slightly on the diagonal. Fill the shape with the color you want using the **PAINT BUCKET** tool. Follow this same process to insert several more squares and align them vertically. To add a picture to the filmstrip squares, click the **EFFECTS >> FILL WITH TEXTURE OR COLOR** command and then choose **PICTURE**. Select the picture to insert. Do this for each of the filmstrip rectangles.

Wakeboarding
SOFTWARE: PS
FONTS: AL Highlight, AL ModernType
Cut out a precise part of an image: Open the photo you want to crop and then click the **MAGNETIC LASSO** tool. (Make sure to feather the tool two pixels for a realistic looking cutout.) Trace around the part of the photograph you want to crop. Click the cut part of the photograph and then press **Ctrl+J** to place the cut image on its own layer. Drag and drop the image onto your layout page.

Color
SOFTWARE: PS
FONTS: AL Highlight, Modern Type, Times Roman
Use the ERASER tool to add an edge to a photograph: Click the **ERASER** tool and then choose the photo edge brush you want to use as an eraser. If needed, adjust the size and opacity of the brush. 100% opacity will give you a complete eraser. To draw the frame, click around the inside edges of the entire photograph.

Refresh
SOFTWARE: PSP
FONTS: Franklin Gothic Medium, AL Songwriter, Placard Condensed, Plastique
Use the DROPPER tool to pick up colors from a picture: Click the **DROPPER** tool and click in the picture the color you want to pick up. (You may have to move the mouse around and view the selected color until you find the one you want.) When you see the color you want, click the left mouse button to place the color in the Foreground and Stroke Properties color palette or click the right mouse button to place the color in the palette for Background and Fill Properties. You can then use this color for other papers and embellishments in the layout. In this example, Anne used the orange from the wood chips, the blue from the sky, and the green from the grass.

2 be Ella at Two
SOFTWARE: PS
FONTS: Carpenter, Garamond, Haettenschweiler
Tint photographs using gradients: To tint the large photo, drag the photo onto a new layer with a white background. Transform the image to black and white and then rotate the image as needed. Create orange horizontal (from left to right), orange vertical (from bottom to top), and green horizontal (right to left) linear gradients. To use the **GRADIENT** tool, select the foreground color. Next click at the start and then drag about halfway to the end point to add the gradient. In the Layers palette, apply the Overlay Blending mode to the two vertical linear gradients. Change the small photograph to black and white and rotate it. To highlight the image in the small photograph, apply two pale yellow radial gradients.

Think
PAPER & ACRYLIC LETTERS: AL
TRANSPARENCY: CI
CONCHOS: Scrapworks
RUB-ONS: KI Memories
DINGBATS: Saru's Flower Dings
Add and emboss special characters: Use the **TYPE** tool to add the flower dingbats to the photo's background. To "emboss" the flowers, rasterize the type layer, apply the Emboss filter, and smooth the edges with a Gaussian blur of 3.0 pixels. To create a transparency, change the blend mode from normal to hard light in the Layers palette. You can then print and use the transparency in your paper based layouts.

My Favorite Place
SOFTWARE: PI
FONTS: AL Patriot, AL Worn Machine, 4990810
Draw shapes and frame photos: To create the orange circle, draw the shape with the **PATH DRAWING** tool, apply a drop shadow, and then fill the shape with a stamp using a custom brush. Follow the same process to add the brown tags but also add text to the tags. Select an edge frame from the frame gallery to blend the large photograph into the background paper. For the small photograph, use the 2D frame to create a white border. Finally, use the **TRANSFORM** tool to rotate this photo.

Light
SOFTWARE: PS
Remove an object or the background from a photograph: Hold down the Alt key and click the **CLONE** tool on a part of the photograph that is about the same color and has the same light tones as the spot you want to replicate. Click on the object or background area you want to remove. Continue to Alt+click and then click to replace the image or background. The background won't be smooth; it will need blending. To smooth the background, use the **HEAL** tool. Hold down the Alt key and click on a spot that is about the same color and has about the same light tones as the spot you want to replicate. Then click on the area to blend. To finish the photograph, copy the photograph layer and paste it so you have two photograph layers. Change the opacity to 70 percent for the top photograph and to 50 percent for the bottom photograph.

Wedding Album
SOFTWARE: PS
PHOTOGRAPHY: Vanderbeek Images
Crop photos to create a collage of several images: Choose the background photograph and then use the **CROP** tool to crop. Crop the smaller photos, cropping out distracting elements and focusing on the area you want to highlight. Drag and drop the smaller photos over the large image, moving and resizing as needed.

CHAPTER THREE

The Myth of Fingerprints
SOFTWARE: PS
FONT: Chalet Book
PAPER: 7Gypsies, KI Memories
STICKERS & RUB-ONS: AL
FRAMES: Pebbles, Deluxe Designs
Create a brush from a fingerprint: Stamp a fingerprint with black ink on white cardstock. Scan the image into Photoshop and convert it to black and white. Use the scan to create a **CUSTOM BRUSH**. To use the brush, select a brush size and "stamp" onto the photograph. (Here Tina used a large brush and stamped it in white three times to create the feel of someone actually applying a fingerprint. She also stamped smaller versions of the fingerprint in gray and black, printed these on a transparency and fit them into the frames.)

Old News
SOFTWARE: PS
FONTS: AL Old Royal, AL Worn Machine
Create patterned paper from a newspaper style custom brush: Scan several different pages from the newspaper at 300 dpi. Select a section of the paper with the **MARQUEE** tool and copy and paste into a new image. Create a new **BRUSH** from this document. Repeat this same process to create several different brushes. Once you've created the brushes, you can use them to create patterned paper.

Snow
SOFTWARE: PS
FONT: AL BoogieWoogie
Use a brush to tint photos: Copy the photograph you want to tint and convert the copy to black and white. Drag the duplicate photo onto the color photo. Apply a Layers mask to the black-and-white photo layer and activate the layers mask. Select a feathered brush and the brush opacity. (An opacity value lower than 50% creates a more nostalgic look. This image has a 100% opacity value so that the color is vibrant.) Make sure the default color palette is selected. **BRUSH** over the areas where you would like color to show through, changing the size of your brush to control the amount of detail. The black brush pulls the color through the layers mask and white brush brings the black-and-white photo back through. This process is similar to erasing, but it allows you to correct mistakes easily by simply shifting between the black and white **BRUSHES**.

Products without a credit are either part of the artist's personal stash or not available for purchase. Note: Unless otherwise noted, all computer fonts are downloaded from the Internet. 2Peas fonts are downloaded from www.twopeasinabucket.com and CK fonts are from Creating Keepsakes.

INDEX 01 HOW TO'S & CREDITS

What Must You Think?
SOFTWARE: PS
FONTS: AL Meaningful, AL Charisma, AL Highlight, AL Outdoors, Times New Roman, Century Gothic, Selfish
Use custom brushes to create patterned papers and to blend photos: To create the red-patterned rectangle, draw the shape, apply a canvas texture using the Texturizer filter, and apply a layer mask by clicking the Layer Mask button in the Layers palette. Click the **PAINT BRUSH** tool and choose a custom brush. Make sure the layer mask is selected (vs. the actual layer) and then draw with the brush. The brush erases the red layer to reveal the turquoise layer beneath. To create the main photo, merge two images by opening the images and de-saturating the color so that both images are black and white. Drag and drop both images onto the layout. Use the **EDIT >> TRANSFORM** command to flip or rotate the image as needed. Next, position one image so it is slightly overlapping the other. Increase the opacity of one image slightly. Apply a Layer Mask to both images. Choose a basic round **BRUSH** with a soft edge, make sure the layer mask is selected and then use the brush to blend the edges, adjusting the opacity of the strokes as you go. For the other faded photos, transform the images to black and white and make any changes needed using the **CURVES** and **LEVELS** tools. Increase the opacity of the image layer and add a Soft Light blending mode to each image. Blend any remaining harsh edges by applying the Layer Mask and using a brush.

Boy
SOFTWARE: PS
FONT: AL Professor
PAPER: AL
TRANSPARENCIES: Magic Scraps, CI
Create custom brushes from household objects: Scan images of textures you find around your house, such as crumpled Saran Wrap or feathers, and use these scanned images to create custom brushes. After you create the **BRUSH**, sweep it over the photo edges or the background. (EXTRA: Joanna typed the text in different layers, added after the brushed border, and varied the opacities and sizes of the text so it looked more like carefree handwriting than computer-generated text.)

Watching the Sunset
SOFTWARE: PSP
FONTS: Bickley Script, Steelfish, Sandra Oh, Plastique, Dymo
Use brushes to "stamp" on patterns to create custom paper: To create the background, use the **FLOOD FILL** tool to fill the area with a tan color. Brush over the background in lighter and darker shades of tan using a grunge brush at low opacity. On a new, transparent layer, use the **PAINT BRUSH** tool to stamp on the "bull's eye" pattern. To draw the "stamp" pattern, start by using a standard round brush to draw large tan circles. Next use a custom "donut" brush to draw the inner burgundy circles. Use a smaller donut brush to add the turquoise circle. To distress the bull's-eye pattern, use the **ERASER** tool with a crosshatch or a grunge brush at a low opacity.

Chilling Out
SOFTWARE: PS
FONTS: Goudy Old Style, AL Professor
Download brush tips: For fast loading and better system performance, create a new Brushes folder in your My Documents folder. To access the **BRUSHES** in this folder, select **REPLACE BRUSHES** from the **BRUSHES** menu. In the dialog box that appears, use the drop-down list to change to the Brushes folder.

If You Know
SOFTWARE: PS
FONTS: AL Afternoon Delight, AL Highlight, Times New Roman
Use a brush to age a photograph: Drag the photo onto a new layer with a white background and transform the image to black and white using the **IMAGE >> ADJUSTMENTS >> DESTURATE** command. Sharpen the photo with the **GRADIENT MAP** tool and then apply a sepia tone with the **IMAGE >> ADJUSTMENTS >> COLOR BALANCE** command. Click the **ERASER** tool, select a brush and then stamp over the photograph to distress it.

Art
SOFTWARE: PS
FONT: AL Highlight
Create brushes from photos or scans: Scan or take photos of interesting textures such as wood, peeling paint, fences, cement, dirt, scratches or fabrics. You can also create a drawing or doodle and use it as the basis for a **BRUSH**. Finally, you can photograph personal items and use them to create brushes. Here Rhonna painted Picasso's name and used it to create a custom brush. To create the brush, adjust your contrast and then select the parts you want to use as the brush. (Erase the background if it is distracting.) Use the **SELECT ALL >> EDIT >> DEFINE BRUSH** command to add the **BRUSH** to your palette.

Inside The Lines
SOFTWARE: PSE
brush: To create the custom brush, create a new layer and then use the **TYPE** tool to type the text or character(s) for the brush. (Here Gina used a large dingbat.) Click **EDIT >> DEFINE BRUSH** to create the brush. Then to use the brush to create a patterned paper, open the background and add a layer. (To add a new layer, click **LAYER >> NEW >> LAYER**.) Click the **BRUSH** tool, click the drop-down arrow to display the available brush styles, and finally select your custom brush. Select the color for the brush and then create your own paper by clicking the **BRUSH** tool on the background.

Happiness
SOFTWARE: PS
FONT: AL Sandra
Use brushes to create custom paper and stamp on design accents: For a distressed or shabby background, use **BRUSHES** as colored brushes, dodge and burn tools, and erasers, concentrating on the edges of the paper. Use text (here "measure happiness") or even a single letter (here "A") as a brush to stamp on design accents. Finally, use the Circle brush as a burn tool to "burn" the shape into the background.

Contact Cards
SOFTWARE: PS
FONT: Kindergarten
Create a brush from a hand-drawn image: Scan hand-drawn images and use to create **BRUSHES** in Photoshop. Create a new document the size of a business card. Add color to the background and then use the brush to place the drawn image. Use the **TYPE** tool to add text.

Suzanne
SOFTWARE: PS
FONTS: Attic, A&S Swan
PAPER: Jennifer Collection, Chatterbox
SNAPS & RIBBON: MM
CHARM & EPOXY LETTER: Li'l Davis Designs
Use a photograph to create a brush: Open the photograph and click **IMAGE >> ADJUSTMENTS >> HUE/SATURATION**. Desaturate the image by adjusting the Saturation level. Adjust the contrast by clicking **IMAGE >> ADJUSTMENTS >> BRIGHTNESS/CONTRAST** and adjusting the Contrast level. Select the image, just inside the existing boundaries, and set the Feather option to 10px. Copy the selected image, open a new image, change the image background to transparent, and then paste the image. Click the **ERASER** tool and select a spatter brush. Use the **BRUSH** to click and erase either the bright or dark areas, depending on the look you want. To save the brush, click **EDIT >> DEFINE BRUSH PRESET** and type a name. You can then use this same brush for other layouts.

That Look
SOFTWARE: PS
FONTS: AL Morning, AL Sandra
Create a cut out text title: In a new image, select the **TYPE** tool, type the title. Create a **BRUSH: SELECT ALL >>EDIT >> DEFINE BRUSH**. Select this title **BRUSH** as an eraser at 100% opacity. Stamp title into the photo layer. Add a drop shadow to the photo for depth.

Brothers
SOFTWARE: PS
FONTS: AL Afternoon Delight, Goudy Old Style, Felix Titling
Adjust the contrast of your photos: Convert your image to black and white by selecting **IMAGE >> ADJUST >> DESATURATE**. Adjust the contrast and brightness levels so that the photo is very white by clicking **IMAGE >> ADJUST >> LEVELS** and making appropriate changes. After you lighten the image, you may notice that some areas remain either too dark or too light. Click the **DODGE/ BURN** tool, select a soft round brush, and reduce the opacity. Then brush over the area you want to lighten or darken. Adjust the opacity of the effect to get an effect that is not too harsh or artificial.

Walking with Butters
SOFTWARE: PS
FONT: AL Class Act, 2peas Submarine, AL Uncle Charles
DINGBAT: 2Peas RP Dangbats
Use dingbats to stamp a pattern: For the background, start with a plain blue color, stamp a pattern (using white with a 20% opacity), and then type the text (also in white). You can print the background on scrapbook sized paper. To create the small picture frame, select a **BRUSH** and "stamp" the dingbat on a plain white background. You can then print the paper, cut out a frame and adhere the stamped frame to a photo. Attach the framed photo and printed title to the background page.

CHAPTER FOUR

Cousins
SOFTWARE: PS
FONTS: AL Highlight, AL Outdoors
Apply a light mode: You can apply a light mode to the background, text or layout elements. In the Layers palette, click **NORMAL** and then **COLOR BURN**. Adjust the opacity level as needed. In this example, Rhonna used an overlay light mode in various opacities on initials, words and flowers in the background. Note that the colors used and how they interact make a

big difference in the final result.

Sweetness
SOFTWARE: PS
FONTS: AL Serenade, AL Playbook, Goudy Old Style
Blend a photo with the background: In the layers window, select the photo that you want to blend with your background. Then click **LIGHT MODE >> PIN LIGHT**. If needed, make additional adjustments to the photo. For instance, use the **DODGE** and **BURN** tools to alter the contrast.

Focus
SOFTWARE: PS
FONTS: AL Afternoon Delight, AL Messenger, AL Outloud, AL Delight, AL Any Time, Century Gothic
Use linear light to increase contrast of photos: Open both images and transform them to black and white using the Desaturate or Gradient Map filter. Drag and drop them to the page. To apply Linear Light mode to both images, select the photo layer in the Layers palette and then select **LINEAR** from the drop-down menu. Make any adjustments. To adjust the exposure of the image, for instance, use the **CURVES** or **LEVELS** tool. Apply a Layer mask and use the **PAINT BRUSH** tool, changing the opacity of the brush, to blend (erase) the edges of the photo.

Split Shift
SOFTWARE: PS
FONT: Arial
PAPER: KI Memories
Merge two photos and adjust the contrast: Take two photos of the same scene at daylight and at night. Heighten the nighttime photograph by using the **BURN** tool to bring out the orange hues. Use the **IMAGE >> ADJUSTMENTS** command to lower the brightness (here 10 percent). Crop the photo in half and then paste it on top of the other photograph. Add text at the seam ("split shift") to make the switch appear seamless.

Time Flies
SOFTWARE: PS
FONTS: AL Messenger, AL Constitution
LABELS: Gina Cabrera, www.DigitalDesignEssentials.com
STAPLES: The Shabby Princess, www.TheShabbyPrincess.com
Use a light mode to create a patterned paper: Draw a rectangle with the **RECTANGLE** tool. Open up a close-up photo of the image you want to use (here a clock). Desaturate and adjust the contrast for the image. Drag and drop the photo onto the layout document and resize it so that it fits into the rectangle you added. Change the **LIGHT MODE** to Soft Light. Follow this same process to create the background for the second page.

Home
SOFTWARE: PS
FONTS: Times New Roman, AL Singsong
Use Screen mode to enhance photos: Drag and drop the main photo to your layout. Desaturate the image to convert it to black and white. Apply auto color to make the black and white more vivid. Select the **BLENDING >> SCREEN MODE** command. Finally, use the **GRADIENT** tool with a green foreground and a yellow background to apply a gradient to the photograph. For the other "faded" photographs, add them to the page, resize them as needed, inverse the selection, and use the **FEATHER** command to soften the photo edges. Apply Screen mode to the smaller photographs and place them under the large main photograph so that they show through and all blend together well.

Unbelievable
SOFTWARE: PS
FONTS: AL Updated Classic, Delight, Times
KIT: "Cabaret" by Rhonna Farrer (included on CD)
Apply an overlay light mode: Start by adding text, photos, brushes and elements on separate layers. Then apply the Overlay mode from the **LIGHT MODE** on the Layers palette; click **NORMAL >> OVERLAY**. If needed, adjust the opacity. Overlay light modes affect any layers underneath the overlay layer, creating depth and various looks.

Wish
SOFTWARE: DIP
FONTS: Kumquat ITC, Johann Sparkling ITC
Touch up photographs with DODGE and BURN brushes: Select either a color or black and white photo to touch up. In this project, the color photograph was first converted to black and white using the **EFFECTS >> BLACK AND WHITE** command and then touched up. To use the **DODGE** and **BURN** brushes to add more contrast to the image, click **TOUCHUP >> OTHER PHOTO REPAIR >> DODGE & BURN BRUSH** and select the brush size, style and settings. Use the **DODGE** brush on overly dark areas and the **BURN** brush to darken overly bright areas or to reveal more detail in washed-out areas.

CHAPTER FIVE

Tricks
SOFTWARE: PS
FONTS: 2Peas Woodpecker, Serifa BT
PAPERS & RUB-ONS: AL
BRADS: American Crafts
Apply a blue filter: Open the photos and then apply the Monday Morning (blue) filter from the Nik Color Efex! Pro Photo Design set. Resize the photograph as needed and then print.

Everything
SOFTWARE: PS
FONTS: Baskerville Old Face, Velvet
Soften skin tons with a filter: Select the color from the background that you want to use for your glow. Make a duplicate layer of your photo. Then click **FILTER >> DISTORT >> DIFFUSE GLOW**, make any changes to the settings, and apply the filter. Next click **FILTER >> BLUR >> GAUSSIAN BLUR** and choose a blur of somewhere between 3 and 5 pixels. Change the Light mode to Lighten and duplicate the layer. In the new layer, change the Layer mode to Multiply and reduce the opacity to 50%. If needed, experiment with the colors using the **IMAGE >> ADJUSTMENT >> HUE/SATURATION** command. After you are satisfied with the colors, add color to the cheeks and lips and lighten (or darken) any parts of the image as needed.

1968
SOFTWARE: PI
FONTS: AL Old Remington, AL Highlight, AL Outloud
Add edge effects to a photo: Open the photograph you want to frame. Click **FORMAT >> FRAME AND SHADOW** and then choose a frame style from the list. In this project, Jeri selected the Edge Frame Gallery for the picture border.

'52
SOFTWARE: PS
FONTS: AL Outdoors, AL Old Remington
Use a plug-in filter: The Neat Image filter makes the images sharper and reduces the noise associated with the film grain in scanned slides and negatives, overcompressed JPEG images, and color banding. To apply this filter, click **FILTERS >> NEAT IMAGE** and make any adjustments. Each photo will be different, so experiment by adjusting the settings for **STRENGTH, PRESERVE DETAILS, REDUCE COLOR, REDUCE NOISE** and **SHARPEN DETAILS**. Note: You can find some free filters online (try www.neatimage.com) as well as purchase filters from companies such as AutoFX and The Plug-in Site.

Shine
SOFTWARE: PS
FONT: AL Cantabile
Apply a Lens Blur filter: Click **FILTERS >> BLUR >> LENS BLUR** and then click OK to apply the default filter. This setting provides small "catch lights" in the eyes. For more blur, adjust the **BLUR FOCAL DISTANCE** and the **IRIS RADIUS, SHAPE, ROTATION,** and **BLADE CURVATURE** to enhance any "catch lights" that already exist in your photo.

The First Moments
SOFTWARE: PS
FONTS: Times New Roman, AL Sandra
Use blur filters: For the photo on the blue background, open the image and duplicate it. Use the **MAGNETIC LASSO** tool to trace and select the main image. Then copy and paste this image to a new layer. Select the first layer and apply a Zoom blur by selecting **RADIAL BLUR** from the **FILTERS** toolbar. Change the default settings to Zoom to blur any distracting background and give the impression of motion. (TIP: The amount of blur will vary with each photo. The trick is to blur it enough to give the impression of motion but not so much that the edges of the subject appear unnatural. You may need to clean up any jagged edges using the **LAYER >> MATTING >> DEFRINGE** command.) Apply a Gaussian blur of 3-5 pixels. Clean up any stray pixels by adding a Layer mask and selecting a soft round brush. For the background photos, open the image, duplicate it and then desaturate the copy. Drag and drop the image to the layout and resize as needed. Apply the Hard Light mode from the Layers palette, adjust the curves and increase the opacity to preference as needed. You may also want to apply a Gaussian blur of a few pixels.

Art Faces
SOFTWARE: PS
FONTS: BlueCake, Carbonated Gothic
Enhance photos with a plug-in filter: Download the filter plug-in from the Internet and install into Photoshop's plug-in directory. For the smaller photos, crop them to the size you want and then use the Virtual Photographer filter to change to either a sepia tone or an enhanced color tone. For the larger photo, use the Virtual Photographer filter to change to an enhanced color tone. Drag and drop all these photos onto the layout document and arrange.

Leaving DC
SOFTWARE: PS
Apply an AutoFX edge to photos: Open the photo in AutoFX. Click **PHOTOGRAPHIC >> EDGES**, select **OUTSIDE EDGE**, and then select **CATALOG**. From the **CATALOG** menu, choose the volume and section to display thumbnails of the available edges. Select the edge you want to apply by clicking it and then clicking OK. Adjust the position of the edge by dragging from the sides. Make any changes you want to the edge by using any of the features in the Edges palette. Save the image and close the AutoFX program. Open your new edged image in

INDEX 01 HOW TO'S & CREDITS

your photo-editing software.

Hypnotized
SOFTWARE: PS
FONTS: Times New Roman, AL Worn Machine, AL Highlight
Add texture with the Noise filter: To create the large tinted photo, drag the photo into your layout and then duplicate that layer. Select the top layer and then saturate the photograph using the **IMAGES >> ADJUSTMENTS >> HUE/SATURATION** command. Use the **MAGNETIC LASSO** tool to select the head and then invert the selection and press the Delete key. This action will erase everything on that layer but the selected area. Select the duplicate layer and desaturate it using the **IMAGES >> ADJUSTMENTS >> DESATURATE** command. Modify the curves as needed using the **IMAGES >> ADJUSTMENTS >> CURVES** command. When both layers are displayed, the head should be saturated and the neck and collar area should appear in black and white. Click **FILTER >> NOISE >> ADD NOISE** and add the amount of noise as desired. You can also add noise using the same command to the text layer.

Spain
SOFTWARE: PS
FONTS: AL Fantasy Type, Times
Use a filter to apply a dreamy effect: You can use built in as well as plug-in filters to apply a filter. In this project, Rhonna applied AutoFx's Dreamy filter (available at www.autofx.com) to the photographs. To apply the filter, click **FILTERS >> DREAM SUITE** and then select the filter (here **SOFT GHOSTING**). Click **OK** to apply the filter.

Everyday Princess
SOFTWARE: DIP
FONTS: Abadi MT Condensed Light, P22 Typewriter, Porcelain
Apply a diffused glow to a photo: Open the photo you want to modify and then click **EFFECTS >> ALL FILTERS**. Click the drop-down list box to display the Photographic filters and then select **GLOW: DIFFUSED**. If needed, customize the settings by clicking **CHANGE ADVANCED OPTIONS**. You can experiment with the setting to your liking. Click Done after you make your selections.

Incomparable
SOFTWARE: PSP
FONTS: AmerType, Century Gothic, Bell
Apply a Soft Focus filter to a photo: Open and copy the photo you want to use. If needed, adjust the contrast, brightness and saturation. Duplicate the photo on a second layer and apply the Soft Focus filter to the second layer. Adjust the Focus and Halo settings, using the preview window to see how your photo will look, and click **OK** when you're happy with the settings. To lessen the soft focus and to allow the bottom photo to show through, decrease the opacity of the second layer to 50%. Merge the two layers and then copy and paste the photo onto the layout.

CHAPTER SIX

Blessed
SOFTWARE: PS
FONTS: AL Updated Classic, Times
KIT: "Forever" by Rhonna Farrer (included on CD)
Recolor paper from a kit: Open your patterned paper from your kit. Use the **IMAGE >> ADJUSTMENTS >> RECOLOR** options (**COLOR BALANCE or REPLACE COLOR**) to change the colors in the paper. Select the **EYE DROPPER** tool and click on the color you want to replace. Change the **HUE REPLACEMENT, SATURATION REPLACEMENT** and **LIGHTNESS REPLACEMENT** settings as needed.

3 in the Snow
SOFTWARE: PS
FONTS: AL Keyboard, AL Oxygen, AL Uncle Charles
PAPERS: Gina Cabrera, www.DigitalDesignEssentials.com
Create background papers with shapes and filters: Create a striped patterned paper by creating varying width strips of color using the **RECTANGLE** tool. Use **FILTER >> DISTORT >> OCEAN RIPPLE** to create a distressed look for the strips. Merge these layers together and then duplicate until the paper's pattern is repeated throughout. Save your paper and use it when you want in any of your layouts.

Temptation
SOFTWARE: PS
FONT: Kravitz
Create background papers using shapes and textures: To draw the squares or rectangles, use the **RECTANGLE** tool. You can select modifications, such as a rounded square, by clicking the appropriate tool option. To draw circles or ovals, use the **ELLIPSE** tool. To draw a perfect square or circle, hold down the Shift key as you draw. To give your shapes texture, make sure that you create new layers for your shapes. Then, in a new top layer, import or create a texture. Change the Layer mode to Overlay or Soft Light. Use the same technique to superimpose photos on only parts of your shapes.

This Face
SOFTWARE: PS
FONTS: Century Gothic, American Typewriter
PHOTOS: Kennady Waldron
Create digital tags: Choose a selection of different papers for the tag. From the first piece of "paper," select the foreground section of the tag using the **RECTANGULAR MARQUEE** tool to draw a rectangle for the tag. Press Ctrl+J to place the shape onto its own layer. Select the background paper for the tag. Select the **CUSTOM SHAPE** tool in the tool palette and the **ROUNDED RECTANGLE** tool from the drop-down menu. Draw the rectangle over the paper; it fills with color. Select the shape and create a new layer for it. Drag and drop these layers onto layout. Line them up and resize them as needed. Using the **ELLIPTICAL MARQUEE** tool, delete a circle in the background paper of the tag. Add white paper strips using the **RECTANGULAR MARQUEE** tool.

Family
SOFTWARE : PS
FONTS: AL Roselyn, Arial
CIRCLE BRUSH:
"Round & Round" Digital Kit, www.twopeasinabucket.com
TRANSPARENT FLOWERS:
"Pea Blossom" Digital Kit, www.twopeasinabucket.com
BLACK EPOXY:
"PEAce Out" Digital Kit www.twopeasinabucket.com
Use digital transparency elements: Open a new image with a transparent background. Using the **CUSTOM SHAPES** tools, draw your shape. In the Layers palette, adjust the opacity to 2-3%. Select the **MAGIC WAND** tool to highlight the outline of your shape. Then create a new layer, adjust the stroke color and size, and apply a blur filter. Create another new layer, select a brush, and stamp on image. Merge the layers with the **LAYERS >> MERGE VISIBLE LAYERS** command. If you want to use the same effect again, save the document as a .PNG file.

Time of Your Life
SOFTWARE: PSE
FONTS: The Bends, 2Peas Tasklist, Century Schoolbook, Plastique
Create metal alpha charms: Create a new small transparent layer at 300dpi. Using the **HORIZONTAL TYPE** tool, add a letter using any desired font. To create the charm loop, click the **CUSTOM SHAPE** tool, select **CIRCLE FRAME SHAPE** from the **SHAPE** drop-down menu, and then draw the circle. Resize and position the circle, if needed, so that it is on top of the letter. Click **LAYER >> MERGE VISIBLE** to lock your two pieces together. To add the "metal" effect, add a Gradient Effect. Use the **GRADIENT** tool options to select **METALS**. Then draw a diagonal line across your page to fill the letter with a gradient. To add some dimension to the charm, display the Layers Styles tab and select **BEVELS >> SIMPLE BEVELS** from the drop-down menu.

Christmas Aspnes Collection 2004
SOFTWARE: PS
FONTS: Undo 35, AL Fantasy Type, AL Delight, Hootie, Diomedez
Create digital picture stamps: In a new document, use the **CUSTOM SHAPE** tool to select a stamp shape. Draw the shape. (TIP: Change the color of the shape to white using the **COLOR PICKER** tool and then rasterize the shape to make it easier to work with.) Open a photo, duplicate it, desaturate the copy to black and white, and make any necessary contrast adjustments. Drag and drop the image onto the stamp shape. Add texture to the image by using one of the existing textures in Photoshop or create your own. Apply a Layer Mask to the photo and use custom distressed brushes to erase the edges of the image. Add any words, letters or numbers using the **TEXT** tool. Double click the Background Layer in the Layers palette and increase the opacity to 0% to create a transparent background. Save the stamp so you can use it in any layout.

Your Day of All Days
SOFTWARE: PS
FONTS: New Century Schoolbook, Powderfinger Type, Dateline, Dirty House, Hootie
PAPERS: KI Memories
RUB-ONS: AL
BRUSH: Grunge brush by Eduardo Recife, www.misprintedtype.com
Use a transparency as the background: Create a background with green numbers on white and then apply a grunge number brush, in black, in front of and behind the numbers. Print this image, as well as the title, on a transparency. In your paper layout, cut out a space for the transparency in your cardstock. Enclose the transparency between the cardstock and the photos and journaling.

12
SOFTWARE: DIP
FONTS: Myraid, Steelfish, Weltron Urban
Create a jewelry tag: Insert a rounded square shape by clicking **INSERT >> SHAPE** and then choosing the appropriate shape. Resize the corners of the square to create a rectangle. Delete the outline by clicking **FORMAT >> SHAPE OR LINE >> LINE THICKNESS** and selecting **NONE**. Next insert a circle shape, resize it, and position the shape on the top of your rectangle. To add the hole for the tag, select a small circle with the **MARQUEE** tool and press Delete. To fill the tag with a selected

background paper, click **EFFECTS >> FILL WITH TEXTURE OR COLOR >> PICTURE** and then select the paper to use. (TIP: To create one object from all of the shapes, group and lock them by pressing Ctrl+A.)

Lollipop Love
SOFTWARE: PSP
FONTS: Boris Black Boxx, Baskerville Old Face, IM Fell Pica
Create a pattern by stamping with a brush: Fill the background with your chosen color at 100% opacity. Use the **PAINT BRUSH** tool to stamp the pattern on a new layer. Here Anne used a custom flower brush for the pattern. She created this brush by using one of Paint Shop Pro's preset floral shapes and by hand drawing the stem and leaves with the **LINE** tool. As you stamp, change the rotation of the brush to create a random pattern. On a third layer, use a crosshatch brush to brush over the entire design with white at a low opacity. With the same brush, use the **ERASER** tool at a low opacity to brush over the white and lower the opacity to 50%. (Portions of the crosshatch remain resulting in a subtle pattern that almost creates the look of linen texture.) After you finish the third layer, merge the three layers together and save your paper. You can then use the paper over and over again.

Nabuta Festival
SOFTWARE: PS
FONTS: AL Dreamboat, Union Agrochem
Use glass styles for elements: To create the decorative "glass" strip, create a new layer and then use the **PAINT BRUSH** tool as a stamp to apply brushwork. (The color used is not important.) Apply a glass style made up of the following layer styles and options: Drop Shadow, Inner Shadow, Bevel & Emboss, and Satin & Gradient Overlay. To create the glass pebble, create a new layer and draw a circle with the **MARQUEE** tool. Fill the circle with color and then apply another glass style. To make the photo appear as though it is enameled, use the **IMAGE >> ADJUSTMENTS >> GRADIENT MAP** command to apply a gradient. Use the **STROKE** tool to change the border of the picture to black with a pixel width of 8–10. Create a new layer and then select a rectangular area using the inner side of the stroke as a guide. Fill the area with any color and then apply a glass style.

Vancouver Aquarium
SOFTWARE: PI
FONTS: AL Patriot, AL Highlight, AL Post Master
Add fibers and string to a layout: Using a custom stamp style with the **STAMP** tool, draw the fibers. Here Jeri drew string closures for the envelope.

The Pumpkin and the Princess
SOFTWARE: PSP
FONTS: Century Gothic, CAC Shishoni Brush, Perpetua
Create a tag with a metal rim and metal brads: On a new layer, use the **ELLIPSE** tool in Circle mode to draw a circle with a gold center and gray border. (Use the **MAGIC WAND** tool to select the gray border.) Click **EFFECTS >> 3D EFFECTS >> INNER BEVEL** to apply an Inner Bevel to the gray border. This command gives the edge a textured, dimensional, metallic look. Next, select the gold with the **MAGIC WAND** tool and use a floral brush in lighter gold to stamp on a subtle pattern. For the initial, type "T" with the **TEXT** tool on a new layer. To create the metal brads, follow the same process, but make the image smaller; in this project, the brad is only 100 pixels wide. Once you create one brad, you can copy and paste it to use it again in the layout.

Determination
SOFTWARE: PI
FONTS: AL Young Crafter, 4990810
Add metallic elements: To create the eyelets, use the **OUTLINE** tool (set to circle) and draw the outline. Then add a metallic preset. To create the brads and staples, use the **PATH DRAWING** tool (set to circle for the brad and rounded rectangle for the staple) to draw the element and then, again, apply a metallic preset. For the metal-rimmed tag, draw the circle with the **CIRCLE** tool, copy it and then switch the mode to **3D PIPE**. As with the other elements, apply one of the program's preset metallic options.

Oh
SOFTWARE: PS
FONTS: Times New Roman, ARDS1, AL Sandra
Use glass styles with text: Type the text (here "let him stay little forever") with the TYPE tool and then apply layer blending options, a drop shadow, inner shadow, and outer glow. For the "Oh," use the **TYPE** tool to type "O" and "H". For the "O", adjust the opacity and position the letter so that it is partially off the page, yet still readable. Duplicate the layer. On the top layer, apply blending options to create the glass look: drop shadow, inner shadow, inner glow, bevel emboss, and stroke.

My Work
SOFTWARE: PS
FONT: AL Post Master
PAPER: AL
STICKERS: American Crafts
Create a transparency: Use the **LEVELS** command to increase the white in the photo. To do so, click **IMAGE >> ADJUSTMENT >> LEVELS** then use the slider bar to make adjustments. Resize and have Kinko's print it on a transparency.

CHAPTER SEVEN

Always Aiden
FONTS: jjstencil, Kravitz Thermal, Lane Narrow, pmn caecilia 55 roman, seeing stars
EYELETS: MM
RUB-ONS: AL
STAMP: Hot Potatoes
Layer text: Using a word processing or photo editing program, create different layers of text in different fonts and sizes and slightly overlap them. Print on white cardstock. To add the star to the photo, open the photo in a photo editing program and create a new layer. Draw the star and use the **TEXT** or **TYPE** tool to type the initial in the middle of the star.

Joy
SOFTWARE: PS
FONTS: Century Gothic, Pharmacy, AL Afternoon Delight
Use shapes or text to create an overlay: To create the dotted overlay, use the **TEXT** tool to type periods, pressing the Tab key or space bar to space the dots. Rasterize the layer, copy it and then move the duplicate beneath the original layer. Merge the two layers so there is now one layer with 2 rows of dots. Duplicate this layer and repeat the process of adding dots until the entire page is covered.

Sisterhood
SOFTWARE: PS
FONTS: AL Cleanliness, AL Featherbrained
LETTER PEBBLES, FLOWERS: Gina Cabrera, *www.DigitalDesignEssentials.com*
Create a "packing-tape" transparency: Crop the photo and drag it onto the layout document. Add a new layer. On this layer, select an area the same size and shape as the photo. Fill the shape with white, add a drop shadow and decrease the fill opacity to 15% to create the transparency. Use custom brushes to erase away portions of the photo, until the image looks similar to a packing tape photo transfer.

Snow Fun
SOFTWARE: PS
FONTS: AL Eyewitness, AL PostMaster
PHOTOS: Vanderbeek Images
Create an overlay to frame photos: On a new layer with a transparent background, create a large rectangle using the **MARQUEE** tool and fill it with color. Add stripes using the same tool and fill with a slightly lighter color. (Note: Keeping each strip on a separate layer will allow you to move them around and change their color.) Using the **CUSTOM SHAPE** tool, create the desired shape, in this case a snowflake. With the Grunge brush, add the same color as the first large rectangle over the shapes and stripes. To make the frames, create a rectangle on a new layer. Fill it with any color. Add a stroke and reduce the fill to 0% so that just the stroke remains. Duplicate that layer.

Thanks
SOFTWARE: ID
FONT: AL Charisma
PAPER: AL
STICKERS: American Crafts
Create an overlay from shapes: Create a text frame and then type or paste journaling into the frame. Use the **RECTANGLE** tool to draw two rectangles and then arrange them so they form a cross. Change the text wrap option so the text wraps around the cross. Print your document on cardstock and cut out the cross area. Arrange your paper and photos beneath the cardstock so they show through the cross.

Amanda
SOFTWARE: PS
FONTS: La Jolla ES, Adobe Caslon Pro, Splendid ES
Change the Light mode: Click on the Light Mode drop-down list in your Layer window. Experiment with different modes for different effects.

The Good Stuff
SOFTWARE: DIP
FONTS: 1942 Report, Beer Dip, BonGuia
PAPERS, BRADS, BOOKPLATE & OVERLAY: Gina Cabrera, *www.DigitalDesignEssentials.com*
Create a text overlay: In a new document, type the words or phrase you want to use as your overlay. If you want to use the same text, you can copy and paste it rather than retype it. Add a background by clicking **INSERT >> PICTURE >> FROM MY COMPUTER** and select the image you want to use. Move the image in back of the text by clicking **FORMAT >> MOVE FORWARD OR BACKWARD >> SEND TO BACK** to move your text to the front. You now have your text overlay that you can use over and over again on any background.

Carefree
SOFTWARE: PSP
FONTS: AL Featherbrained, Kenyan Coffee, Boris Black Boxx, Gigi
Create a floral overlay: Open a new transparent document and use the **FREEHAND SELECTION** tool to draw the outline of the flower. Fill the flower with

85

INDEX 01 HOW TO'S & CREDITS

turquoise using the **FLOOD FILL** tool at 100% opacity. Copy the flower and paste it on a new transparent layer. Use the **DEFORMATION** tool to reduce the size of the second flower to 90% and fill the flower with aqua at 100% opacity. Use the **MOVE** tool to center the smaller flower over the larger flower. Finally, use the **PAINT BRUSH** tool with the standard, circular brush to stamp on a yellow center. Merge the visible layers of the image to keep the background transparent and then add a subtle drop shadow. Copy the flower image and paste it onto the layout on a new transparent layer (in this case, the top layer). To give the layer the look of a true transparency, reduce the transparency of the layer to 85%.

Footsteps
FONTS: AL Afternoon Delight, Times New Roman
Apply a text overlay: Open the text overlay and copy it to a new blank page. Here the text color is white, so Dena also changed the background color, choosing a color from her photo. She also used the **RECTANGULAR MARQUEE** tool to draw and fill other areas with other colors from the photo. You should now have, stacked in order: the background, the rectangle, and the text overlay. Add the photo and resize and reposition it as needed. Drag the photo layer so that is beneath the white lines.

Reflect
SOFTWARE: PS
FONTS: AL Sandra, AL Songwriter
Create an overlay with text in different fonts: Using your **TEXT** tool, type the words or letters you want to include, adjusting the sizes, colors, opacity and rotation of the text. In the Layers palette, link the text layers together and then merge the layers. Save the document as **.PNG** file to keep its transparent qualities.

Enjoy
SOFTWARE: PS & ID
FONTS: AL Modern Type, AL Uncle Charles, MS PMincho, Zapf Dingbats (snowflake)
PAPER & RUB-ONS: AL
Add special characters: To add dingbats to your designs, such as the snowflake dingbat used in this project, add new text layers using the TYPE tool. Adjust the size, color and type of dingbat using the options in the Character palette. Use the Layers palette to change the opacity of the dingbat.

Infatuation
SOFTWARE: PS
FONTS: Chalet New York, Century Gothic, Irezumi
STICKERS & ENVELOPE: Chronicle Books

EPOXY STICKERS: AL
RUB-ONS: KI Memories
RIBBON: MM
Create a "water" transparency: Layer the text over the photo so that the word overlaps the edges of the photo. Copy the text several times so it covers the entire background. Increase the transparency so the photo remains visible in the background and alter the color.

The Real You
SOFTWARE: PS
FONTS: Ameretto, Menuetto
Create a template overlay: Insert your template elements each in a different layer. Change opacities and light modes to get various effects. (Note: Remember to leave plenty of "white space" in the file so you have areas to insert your images and/or text.) Once you have created the overlay, flatten your file and save it as **.PNG** file to maintain the transparency. You can then use this overlay in any layout, varying the Hue/Saturation or the rotation as needed.

Autumn Golf
SOFTWARE: PS
FONTS: AL Landscape, AL Patriot
Add a sheer color block: On a new blank layer, select the **MARQUEE** tool and draw a rectangle over the bottom section. Fill with black. Do the same for the upper section. Reduce the opacity of each black rectangle layer to 50%. Add text to the top using a white font over the top black rectangle. Add the title over the lower black rectangle. Add place and date on the lower left and right over the title in orange.

A Boy and His Ball
FONTS: Serifa BT, Interstate
PAPER, EPOXY STICKERS & RUB-ONS: AL
BRADS: American Crafts, SEI
Create circular text and transparent patterns: In your photo editing program, use the specific features to create circle text. Also draw circles, overlapping squares, and lines to create a pattern. Print these on transparencies, trim to match the circles on the paper layout, and adhere with hidden adhesive or brads.

You at Age Four
SOFTWARE: PS
FONTS: AL Highlight, Circus, Circus Ornate
Create an overlay using photos: Create a new layer and draw a shape for your overlay. Fill the shape with color and adjust the opacity (to around 2%) so that you can see through to the next layer. In a new layer, add your photographs within the overlay shape. Merge the layers together and save the document as a **.PNG** file (which compresses the file size but retains the transparent qualities).

CHAPTER EIGHT

LAX
SOFTWARE: PS
FONT: AL Terzini
PHOTO EDGE: Rhonna Farrer, www.twopeasinabucket.com
BRADS: Karen Foster
METAL LETTERS: American Crafts
Add a photo edge and apply a layer: Open a photo and resize it to 8"x12". Open the photo edge and resize to the same size as the document. Layer the frame over the photo. Add type and then print the photo. Open the same photograph, but resize to 3"x3" and change to black and white. Use the Artistic Colored Pencil filter to change the look of the photo. Print, attach both photos to page, and finally add letter, brads and journaling.

Color
SOFTWARE: PS
FONTS: AL Oxygen, AL Sandra
Use a photo to create a layout title: Open the photo you want to use to create the title. Type the Title using the **TYPE** tool and then position it with the **MOVE** tool. Select the photo layer on the Layer palette and then hold down the Ctrl key and click on the title layer. Click **LAYER >> NEW >> LAYER VIA COPY**. Drag the title onto your layout document and then add drop shadow and texture to complete the look.

Go Speed Racer
SOFTWARE: DIP
FONTS: AL Libretto, Litterbox, P22 Typewriter, 28 Days Later
PAPERS, RIBBONS & METAL RIMMED TAG: Gina Cabrera
www.DigitalDesignEssentials.com
Add a watermark: Insert the text to use as the watermark. Change the color to a slightly darker shade of your background color by clicking **TEXT >> TEXT BOX COLOR >> MORE COLORS**, selecting the color, and clicking **OK**. Select your text box and then click **EFFECTS >> TRANSPARENCY >>EVEN**. Adjust the transparency to a value between 50-75. The sample uses a setting of 70. Position the text on the background or image.

She
SOFTWARE: PS
FONTS: AL Sandra, AL Songwriter
Alter a photo's color: Drag a black-and-white photo onto a colored shape and apply an Overlay Light mode to change the color (here to lavender).

Mini Calendar
FONT: Skia

RUB-ONS: AL, Li'l Davis
Create a mini calendar: Use Excel or a calendar program to create each calendar page. Copy and paste the calendar from the program to your Photoshop document. Add the photos to the pages for each month. To make the calendar parts of the page more visible, click **LAYER >> LAYER STYLE >> DROP SHADOW** to apply drop shadows to the numerals.

Big Wide World
SOFTWARE: PS
FONTS: Century Gothic, Arial, 3 grammes 5
Add curved or spiral text: To add curved text, make sure the **PATH** option is set and then use the **CUSTOM SHAPE** tool to draw the shape. (Hold down the Shift key as you draw.) Select the **TEXT** tool, click the beginning of curved line that extends around the custom shape, and type the text. To create the spiral text, start with a new document and a new layer. Draw and fill a rectangle with black and apply the Twirl filter twice, setting the angle at the highest value. Select everything on the layer (click **SELECT >> ALL**) and copy it. Create a new channel using the Channels palette and then paste the objects to this channel. Open the Paths palette and create a work path. Switch to the Layers palette and delete the swirl layer. With the **DIRECT SELECTION** tool, click on the path to create points. Drag individual selection boxes over the two start points and the point where both spirals converge and delete one of the spirals. Select the **TEXT** tool, click on the spiral, and type your text. After you add the text, delete the work path and drag and drop the spiraled text to your layout.

30 minutes
SOFTWARE: PSP
FONTS: Eurostyle, Hootie!
Add curves and rounded corners to layout elements: To create a curved piece of paper, draw the shape with the **SELECTION** tool set to **ELLIPSE** on a transparent layer. To draw the curve, click off the left edge of the layout and drag the cursor onto the page. Keep dragging right and down until the curved edge of the ellipse stretches from the top of the page to the bottom. Fill the selection with color at 100% opacity, stamp on a pattern with the **PAINTBRUSH** tool, and apply a drop shadow. To create the rounded rectangle, draw the shape with the **SELECTION** tool, set to **ROUNDED RECTANGLE**, on a new layer. Fill the shape with white at 100% opacity and apply a drop shadow. Use the **ROUNDED RECTANGLE** tool again on a new layer to draw the shape of the purple rectangle. Make this rectangle slightly smaller than the white one and fill with

purple at 100% opacity. Stamp on a pattern with the **PAINTBRUSH** tool and apply a drop shadow. Center the purple rectangle over the white one.

Driving Him Crazy
SOFTWARE: PS
STICKERS: American Crafts
Create a brush from a doodle: Scan your doodle and then open the image. Click **EDIT >> DEFINE BRUSH PRESET**. After you have created the custom brush, use it to "stamp" a doodle in white onto a blue background.

Standing Out in the Crowd
FONT: lassigue dmato
PUNCH: Marvy
Overlap text to create a background: Create one layer of the sentence (here "Standing out in the crowd"). Copy and paste the text creating multiple layers of the same phrase. Overlap the phrases to create the background.

Très Chic
SOFTWARE: PS
FONTS: AL Hurried Note, AL Uncle Charles
BRUSH: Rhonna Farrer, www.twopeasinabucket.com
Create a patterned title and photo edges: Use the TEXT tool to type your title. On a new layer, drag and drop the patterned paper to use for the title. To add custom photo edges, create a custom brush from scans of textures, photos or illustrations. Use the brushes to add the edge to the photos.

Holiday Cards
Noel Card
SOFTWARE: PS
FONTS: Carpenter, Carla
Create a Christmas card with background photos: Select the photos for the card and then convert them to grayscale. Use the **IMAGE >> ADJUST >> LEVELS** command to match the brightness, contrast and overall coloring for the photos. Move the photos to the corners of the page, leaving just enough room for the star ornament. Print the card on photo quality cardstock, adhere this page to a red cardstock, and glue the star ornament in the center of the card.

Peace Card
SOFTWARE: PS
FONTS: AL Cantible, Selfish
Brushes: Own design & Rhonna's digital kits, www.twopeasinabucket.com
Use Brushes to create custom Christmas cards: In a New Image, select Custom Brush tools in varying colors. Stamp onto your image canvas, adjusting levels of opacity for depth. Select Type Tool to add some text; for depth, adjust the level of opacity on the "P" to around 15%. Print out, cut with scalloped scissors, adhere to cardstock. For additional embellishments, on a New Image, stamp your Custom Brushes, then, print on inkjet transparency, cut out and adhere with pop dots and brads for some added interest.

Snowman Card
SOFTWARE: PS
FONT: Goudy Old Style
Embellish a drawing: Draw your snowman's arms, hat, scarf, eyes, buttons, and the ground by hand. Use the clear glass marbles to measure the size. Scan the image into your computer and import it into a new file. Add snowflakes using the **SHAPE** tool. Add text and draw a red border around the image. Print this image and use in your paper-based layout.

Circle of Friends
Create a circle book: Cut watercolor paper to the size of circle for your book. Print the back of the book design for both sides and then rip them out so that a rough edge is left. Use ink to age the edges.

The Girl with Kaleidoscope Eyes
SOFTWARE: Kaleider (www.whizical.com)
PAPER: KI Memories
EPOXY: Li'l Davis
Create a kaleidoscope from photos: To create the kaleidoscopes, see if your program has a kaleidoscope effect and apply it, or use a special software program. In this project, Tina used a program called Kaleider to create the images. She opened photos of flowers in the program, adjusted the images, and used a variety of angles and parts of the photos to create multiple versions. She saved the images, cropped and then printed them for use in a paper based layout.

"Honey Do" List
SOFTWARE: PS
FONT: Century Gothic
PHOTO: Marilen Sarian
Create a "To Do" list: Create a new blank document and then use the **RECTANGLE** tool to draw a rectangle. Fill the rectangle with color. Use the **TEXT** tool to type the title using white as the text color. Move the text so it is flush with the bottom of the rectangle. Create the subtitle using the **TEXT** tool and lime green as the text color. Layer the subtitle over the title. Add other text as well as cropped square photos to the bottom of the layout.

What's Better?
SOFTWARE: PS
FONT: Gill Sans MT
BRADS: American Crafts
Create patterned paper: Open a new document and then using the **RECTANGLE** and **ELLIPTICAL** tools, create stripes and circles. Fill the shapes with colors and add borders or outlines. Print on textured cardstock.

Calendar
SOFTWARE: PS
FONTS: Kozuka Gothic Standard, Century Gothic
Create a calendar from a template: Your program may include templates for special documents such as a calendar. You can customize the template, adding your own photos. Open the photos you want to use and crop as needed. Drag and drop the photo to the template. Move the photo layer below the template layer.

Siblings
SOFTWARE: PS
FONTS: AL Afternoon Delight, Goudy Old Style, Felix Titling
Adjust the contrast of your photos: Convert your image to black and white by selecting **IMAGE >> ADJUST >> DESATURATE**. Adjust the contrast and brightness levels so that the photo is very white by clicking **IMAGE >> ADJUST >> LEVELS** and making appropriate changes. After you lighten the image, you may notice that some areas remain either too dark or too light. Click the **DODGE** or **BURN** tool, select a soft round brush, and reduce the opacity. Then brush over the area you want to lighten or darken.

The Patterson Children
SOFTWARE: PS
FONT: AL Anytime
Erase parts of an old photograph: Scan and then open the photograph. Duplicate the photo using the **IMAGE >> DUPLICATE**. Using the **CROP** tool select the person in the photo you want to keep. (You'll create a single portrait of this person.) Start with the largest brush and make sure the brush is featured as much as possible. Holding down the Alt key, click in the area you want to sample from. Then simply brush away the area you do not want. As you work on the image, you may need to change to a smaller brush. Also, continue to resample so that you get even color as you move around the photo.

Serendipity
SOFTWARE: PS
FONTS: Times New Roman, AL Verdigris
Update old photographs: Scan and save the photograph (or other item). Then open the image and adjust the levels and/or curves to clean up the image. Use the Healing brush to repair small scratches or marks on the photos. Press the Alt key and click on the area of the photo to use as a replacement for the scratched or marred area. Apply a Layer mask and Overlay and/or Hard Light modes to blend the photos and images into the background.

Poet
FONT: Bodoni XT
RIBBON: Offray
PUNCH: Marvy
EYELETS & METAL LETTERS: MM
Change a photo's color: Scan in the cover of the book. Use the **RECTANGLE MARQUEE** tool to create a rectangle of orange color over the scanned in image. Reduce the opacity to 65% so the cover shows through but has an orange tint.

Magic
SOFTWARE: PS
FONT: AL Songwriter
KIT: "Cabaret" by Rhonna Farrer (included on CD)
Customize a kit: Open a new document for your layout. Open various elements from the digital kits. Use the **MOVE** tool and drag and drop the kit elements you want to use into your new document. If you need to resize the papers or other elements, click **EDIT >> TRANSFORM >> SCALE**. Hold down the Shift key and drag any of the corners of the element to resize. To recolor an element to match your photos, click **IMAGE >> ADJUSTMENTS >> REPLACE COLOR**. Select the area you want to replace using the **EYE DROPPER** tool and select the new color using the sliders.

Heart
SOFTWARE: PS
FONTS: AL Modern Type, AL Constitution
Recolor paper: To recolor paper, use the Hue/Saturation, Selective Color, or Gradient Map dialog box options, or use a color overlay. Another option, shown here, is to add a fill layer above the paper and change the layer style.

The Art of Life
SOFTWARE: DIP
FONTS: Edition, Classizism Antiqua
Create a basic layout: Create a new file and then add your background paper using **INSERT >> PICTURE >> FROM MY COMPUTER** and selecting your paper. Add text, photos and shapes. Move and resize the elements as needed.

Cutie Pie
FONT: Lane Narrow
RIBBON: Offray, Kate's Paperie, Midori
STICKER: EK Success
SNAPS: MM
Change the color of paper: Using the **RECTANGLE MARQUEE** tool, create blocks of color to overlap existing patterns. Reduce the opacity to roughly 50% and then print to size.

OTHER BOOKS BY AUTUMN LEAVES

Designing with Digital continues the prestigious Autumn Leaves flagship *Designing With* book series, which includes the following titles:

Designing With Vellum

Designing With Notions

Designing With Texture

Designing With Photos

Designing With Words

Designing With Fabric

The Book Book

Designing With Simplicity

Designing With Stamping

Designing With Paper

As our little collection of books has grown, it has affectionately been dubbed the "DW Series". Enjoy your copy of *Designing with Digital,* and keep an eye out for much more in the DW series, coming to a store near you.